Against all Reason

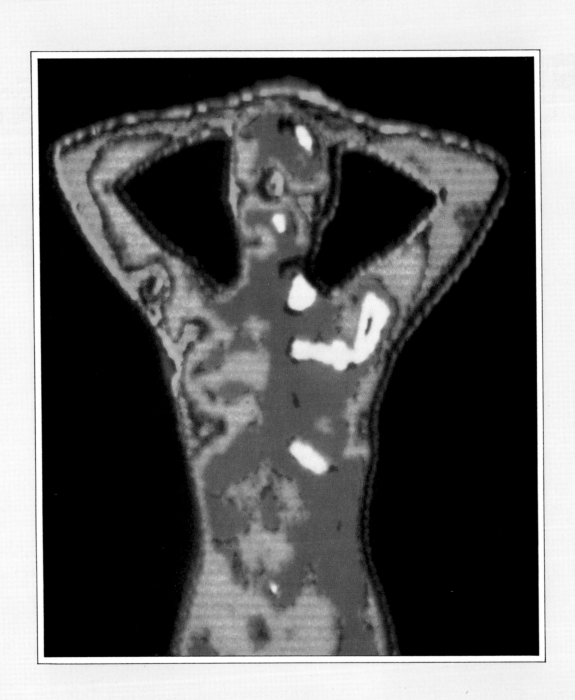

THE Unexplained

Against all Reason

Experimental evidence for the existence of psi

Editor: Peter Brookesmith

Orbis Publishing · London

Acknowledgements

Photographs were supplied by AGA Infrared Systems Ltd, Aldus Archive, Associated Press, J. Beloff, British Museum, Eldon Byrd, Cooper Bridgeman Library, W.E. Cox, J. Cutten, Arnold Desser, Escher Foundation, Mary Evans Picture Library, B.R. Grad, Elmar Gruber, Prof J. Hastad, Toby Hogarth, Brian Inglis, Julian Isaacs, Daniel Kleinz, London Scientific Films, Thelma Moss, National Enquirer, Novosti, Kit Pedler, Photri, Guy Lyon Playfair, Polyclinic Medical Center, Popperfoto, Psi Search, Psychic Magazine, Rex Features, Heath Robinson Estate, Ann Ronan Picture Library, Hassan Salmani, Carl Sargeant, Science Photo Library, Brian Snellgrove, Sorrat, Spectrum, Roy Stemman, Syndication International, Targ & Puthoff/Mind Reach, Thames TV, Jean Guy Thibodeau, John Topham Picture Library.

The illustration on page 92 top is © by SPADEM, Paris 1982.

Consultants to
The Unexplained
Professor A. J. Ellison
Dr J. Allen Hynek
Brian Inglis
Colin Wilson
Editorial Director
Brian Innes
Editor
Peter Brookesmith
Deputy Editor
Lynn Picknett
Executive Editor
Lesley Riley
Sub Editors
Mitzi Bales
Chris Cooper
Jenny Dawson
Hildi Hawkins

Picture Researchers
Anne Horton
Paul Snelgrove
Frances Vargo
Editorial Manager
Clare Byatt
Art Editor
Stephen Westcott
Designer
Richard Burgess
Art Buyer
Jean Hardy
Production Co-ordinator
Nicky Bowden
Volume Editor
Lorrie Mack
Assistants
Ruth Turner
Sarah Reason

Material in this publication previously appeared in the weekly partwork *The Unexplained*, © 1980–83 This edition © Orbis Publishing Ltd, London, 1984

Printed and bound in Yugoslavia by Gorenjski Tisk

Contents

Introduction

SHOULD YOU BE walking down the street and have the misfortune to get your head in the way of a falling steel girder, you would have some reason to call the resulting pain 'mind-bending'. Even in normal circumstances, however, you might be forgiven for deriding the proposition that the reverse might be true: that mind might bend metal. Yet some of the most careful and controlled research in parapsychology in recent years has been directed to discovering whether the mind can, by some means as yet undefined, affect the material world in just this dramatic way.

No less effort, it should also be said, has been expended by sceptics in trying to refute the actuality of metal bending – and other forms of mind-over-matter, known as psychokinesis or PK for short. And more than that – a really dedicated sceptic will deny that even the *possibility* of such an event exists. The logic of this somewhat inflexible thinking is something we'll return to: first, let us take a look at the kind of evidence researchers in the field have been concerned to discover – and at the pitfalls that litter this kind of research.

The 'original' metal bender was, of course, the Israeli Uri Geller (now settled in New York). Geller is worth discussing in detail because his case highlights the popular reaction to psychokinesis, the ways in which scientists approach the problems represented by psi, and the extremely strange people who attach themselves to the whole business of psychical research.

Geller was discovered by the inventor Andrija Puharich in 1971 when the Israeli was working the night club circuit in Tel Aviv with his spoon-bending show. Puharich is a problematic character. He has a string of electrical and electronic patents to his name, the comfortable income from which both testify to his practical and effective common sense in scientific terms, and allow him to indulge his interest in psychic matters. When he does so indulge himself, however, it is difficult to say whether that practical good sense entirely deserts him, or whether in some peculiar fashion he acts as a catalyst and a focus for weird and inexplicable events. Certainly every apparently psychic case that he investigates becomes – according to his own as well as others' testimony – quite baroque in its intensity.

In the case of Geller, whom he can with some justice be said to have started on a career of psychic superstardom, the simple spoon-bender from the Middle East became the centre of truly incredible events: teleportations across the city of New York, sightings of UFOs, communications with the 'Nine' who turned out to be a cosmic committee of 'space beings' taking a persistent, if unobtrusive, interest in world affairs, and more. All very well, perhaps, had the evidence in the form of tape recordings, photographs and the rest not all magically been wiped from tape, film and paper before independent investigators could get near them. And Puharich's account of all this paranormal mayhem did, in the end, work against Geller's reputation, for the simple reason that most people couldn't listen to it with a straight face.

Geller and Puharich parted company in due course, but the publicity had had two effects. Geller came to the attention of a number of scientists who were, in the early 1970s, prepared to investigate claims for the paranormal without prejudice. And he had made a public for himself and for the art – or knack – of apparently bending metal and otherwise affecting material objects by the mind alone.

It is here that the metal bending phenomenon become most difficult to assess. As far as the scientists were concerned, very little that was of any use to them emerged from the time Geller spent in laboratories in Europe and the United States. Much anecdotal evidence was gathered, as machinery broke down inexplicably or simply refused to work while the self-styled 'mentalist' was around, but very little else happened. And in the process one renowned mathematician, Professor John Taylor of the University of London, very nearly ruined his reputation and career. Taylor studied Geller for a while and, as a result of this, and of publishing an open-minded book on the paranormal, was virtually ostracised by his colleagues. In the fullness of time, having got nowhere with Geller or with his other experimental work in psi, Taylor recanted, disowned all connection with parapsychology, and was welcomed back by his peers into the 'sane' and uncontroversial world of science.

As for the public at large, matters were very different. For whenever Uri Geller appeared on television or was heard on radio, people would report that odd happenings were taking place in their homes. Broken clocks and watches would spontaneously right themselves and tick merrily away (though not, very often, for very long). Drawers full of cutlery would twist and bend. People discovered suddenly that they too could twist forks by sheer mind power.

Are they all fooling themselves, or lying, or at the very least making honest mistakes when they report such events? And if they are not, why is it that Geller – and other metal benders – seem to make so little headway under experimental, laboratory conditions?

It's certainly true that virtually any watch, when picked up after a long while not working, will tick for a short time. What is less certain is a) whether the force behind these occurrences is at all similar to the physical forces familiar to science, and b) whether it can be tapped or directed at will. One distinguished psychical researcher in Britain has likened taking a psychic into a laboratory to taking any average person into some cold and solitary place and asking him or her to fall in love for the benefit and illumination of the sages gathered therein. This analogy doesn't quite fit the case, however, for metal benders seem able to perform quite adequately to their own orders if not to anyone else's. And there's no doubt that *certain* psychical researchers consistently get better results than others – if a few, despite their own dearest wishes, fail to get any positive results at all.

It is here that we meet one of the most paradoxical aspects of psychic research – and, as it happens, of advanced research in physics, too. For decades, physicists have recognised that the *very act of observing* an event at the subatomic level will actually affect the behaviour of the thing they are looking at. A number of psychical researchers are now convinced that something like this happens in their own field and have called it the 'experimenter effect'. In sum, it amounts to the fact that a sympathetic observer or experimenter in psi will persistently get more positive results than one who is sceptical – no matter how unconscious that scepticism may be.

Parapsychology thus ends up, as far as mainstream science is concerned, tossing a two-headed coin. For if the experimenter effect does occur, then no truly neutral experimenter is likely to be able to produce – and so prove the existence of – psi effects in his laboratory; and certainly no sceptic will be able to. Believing is seeing. And believers will continue to believe and the militant rationalists will continue to cry that the believers have been hoaxed, are gullible, bad scientists or at worst hoaxers themselves.

So much for the problems that face scientists. The problems that ferocious and determined sceptics have are probably best discussed from the perspective of the psychiatrist's couch, but a word or two of warning seem to be in order. Perhaps the most famous of these self-appointed scourges is James 'the amazing' Randi, who is obsessed with proving that every psychic is a fraud. Randi himself is, there is no doubt, a very accomplished stage magician, illusionist and escape artist. He steps out of his field of knowledge though when he claims that because he can *reproduce* 'psychic' effects and events by sleight of hand, there must be no such thing as genuine phenomena. This is like saying that because a second-rate painter is capable of passing off a deliberate fake of his own as a Picasso, real Picassos do not exist.

For those of us who are prepared to believe that psychokinesis may well be possible, there remains the problem of *how* it happens – what forces there may be at work during such events. Here again there are a variety of differing interpretations and approaches to the question.

Psychical research as we know it today began as a response to Spiritualism. Psychical researchers investigated not only hauntings and apparitions but sundry other peculiar phenomena that were ascribed to spirit forces: poltergeist attacks, for instance, as well as the odd things that happened in Victorian seance rooms, such as table lifting, levitation, and materialisations like ectoplasm. Today, few of these things would automatically be laid at the door of the spirit world. Poltergeists, for example, seem to be strictly psychological in origin, but that doesn't explain *how* a disturbed adolescent (or deeply repressed adult) makes objects crash about. And some investigators are quite happy to suggest that the psychological problem is caused by elementals, (mischievous spiritual entities), who do the actual damage.

One of the most extraordinary histories of psychokinesis began in fact as a kind of Spiritualist experiment in the early 1960s. It had become a matter of controversy and acrimonious debate by the early 1980s, but had also provided parapsychologists with a remarkable investigative tool – and raised searching questions about the source of psi phenomena. The story centres on the SORRAT (Society for Research on Rapport and Telekinesis) group from Rolla, Missouri, and is dealt with fully in the pages that follow. The point to be made here is that although the experiment was started by people who believed that they were confirming the existence of a spirit world of some kind, the evidence that has emerged could just as easily be said to be without intelligent, never mind human, direction, since the phenomena are largely trivial and pointless – if, in their own way, spectacular, rather like an enormous firework display that is without reason or coherence. The most profitable result of the proceedings is probably the invention of the 'mini-lab', a sealed container used as an environment for psi events that can in turn be objectively recorded on film or tape. From the nature of the Rolla material there is, as so often, no *conclusive* evidence that fraud has not been perpetrated, though the characters of the people involved make the likelihood of an elaborate hoax remote.

That leaves us with the perennial problem of the kind of people who involve themselves in research of this kind. Puharich has already been mentioned, but a classic of his kind was the pretentious, misguided and yet probably ultimately sincere investigator Harry Price. He typifies the enthusiastic researcher who, anxious to establish himself and his chosen field as both respectable and exciting, was led into all kinds of blunder, self-deception and possibly even sly encouragement of the evidence. Price has his defenders and his detractors, even today, but there is an irony here for these who suck their teeth and tut-tut loudly at his antics. For there is developing a highly regarded theory of psi actually suggesting that a little hoaxing here and there may not be a bad thing.

Developed by the British researcher Kenneth Batcheldor, the theory says that if you wish to develop psychokinetic occurrences in conditions rather like those of the old seance rooms, the best way to get the phenomena going in the first place is – fake it! Provided that the hoax is always owned up to by the conspirators, this seems to have the remarkable effect of bringing genuinely inexplicable phenomena in its wake.

Against all reason indeed. But the very possibility of psi is against all reason. That is however, no reason why such things should not happen, however inexplicable they have managed to remain so far.

PETER BROOKESMITH

Psi: the secret agent

Are psychic events a common, but concealed, part of everyday life? And, if so, how can they be investigated? JULIAN ISAACS explains how American researcher Rex G. Stanford found answers to these questions

RELATIVELY FEW PEOPLE claim to have had psychic experiences, even fewer to be gifted psychically. But there is a quiet revolution in progress within parapsychology that may radically alter this idea of the rarity of psychic happenings in everyday life. The research involved has shown not only that psychic functioning is much more common than was imagined, but also that it is possible to devise a model on the basis of which themes underlying spontaneous psi may be tested in the laboratory.

The new model of psychic functioning was created by American parapsychologist Rex G. Stanford in 1974. However, the news seems not to have spread beyond parapsychological circles, perhaps because of the

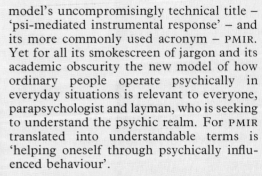

Above: Rex G. Stanford, who discovered PMIR

Below: ESP tests were most successful when targets were accompanied by erotic cards

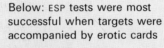

model's uncompromisingly technical title – 'psi-mediated instrumental response' – and its more commonly used acronym – PMIR. Yet for all its smokescreen of jargon and its academic obscurity the new model of how ordinary people operate psychically in everyday situations is relevant to everyone, parapsychologist and layman, who is seeking to understand the psychic realm. For PMIR translated into understandable terms is 'helping oneself through psychically influenced behaviour'.

Self-centred psi

The two main features implicit in the PMIR model are, first, that one usually does something ultimately to benefit oneself and, secondly, that this self-serving activity involves behaviour that has a psychic component. This behaviour can be of various sorts: it can be purely psychic, such as influencing one's surroundings directly by psychokinesis (PK), it can involve influencing the actions of others, or very commonly receiving information through ESP and benefiting from it. People can exhibit all these forms of PMIR behaviour without being aware that they are doing anything psychic whatsoever. This is, by implication, startling; it means that a person's behaviour may demonstrate that he has detected some useful fact or situation through ESP alone – but his experience of the 'real world' leads him to deny the possibility that anything paranormal is responsible.

To establish this point – which is crucial to the PMIR model – evidence must be collected to show that people actually do demonstrate PK or ESP in ways useful to themselves, without the least idea that they

Left: Mrs Jones, who has a gift for being appropriately dressed on every occasion, tried on her 'wedding' hat one day and remarked that it was a long time since she had been to a wedding. The next day her daughter turned up, announcing that she had just become engaged. Mrs Jones wore that same hat to the wedding. PMIR most often works through our everyday motivations – in this case Mrs Jones's preoccupation with suitable dressing

Below: in one American experiment designed to show the existence of hidden ESP, students were given the deliberately boring task of predicting the path of a randomly moving light with a light pen (left). Meanwhile in the next room a female assistant monitored a random event generator – REG – that was acting as a sort of electronic coin tosser (centre); when the REG scored the equivalent of seven heads or tails the students were released from their boring task and allowed to sort pictures of scantily clad women (right). Only about three students should have 'escaped' by chance alone; in fact eight did. It seemed that somehow the students had affected the REG by psychic means

are doing so. This type of effect, which is known as 'non-intentional psi', might seem impossible to research, yet there is an extensive literature dealing with this very subject.

In the laboratory, ESP tests have been camouflaged so that they appear to be normal academic examinations, or what have appeared to be tests of memory have in fact masked tests of ESP. And students without knowing it have scored significantly on the ESP tests. Such experiments show that non-intentional psi is not only possible, but common.

For example, an ESP test was conducted with some American students in 1974 where they had to describe Zener cards that were concealed in opaque sealed envelopes. This, however, was only the intentional ESP task; in fact it acted as a cover for the non-intentional task. Unknown to any of the students, some of the envelopes contained erotic photographs of women as well as the Zener cards. Male college students were found to have scored significantly higher on the ESP cards that were accompanied by the erotic photographs, whereas female college students showed no such bias. When the experiment was repeated with younger pupils the more anxious subjects tended to miss scoring on the targets with the erotic photographs to a statistically significant extent.

No sex, please

This demonstrates two points: one is that people can, and do, behave in a way that is clearly influenced by their receiving information through ESP of which they are consciously unaware, and the second is that the response they make to this information is characteristic of their normal interests and concerns. The female college students showed little reaction to the envelopes containing erotic targets, just as research has shown that girls are much less likely to buy erotic books or magazines than boys. The boys, on the other hand, reacted to the erotic targets much as they would in normal circumstances. It is also consistent with the normal behaviour of the younger pupils that the anxious children should react by avoiding the disturbingly erotic pictures.

Another example of the way in which PMIR behaviour reflects a person's normal interests has a real life setting, rather than a rigidly controlled laboratory one, so that coincidence cannot be ruled out as an explanation. It concerns a rather psychic lady, Mrs Jones, who is unusually well-dressed and possesses a considerable flair for being appropriately dressed for every occasion.

One day she felt moved to sort out a cupboard that she had not thought of for some months. While tidying it she came across several of her hats. Picking out one that was suitable for a wedding she put it on, remarking to her husband that it was a long time since they had attended one. She tried

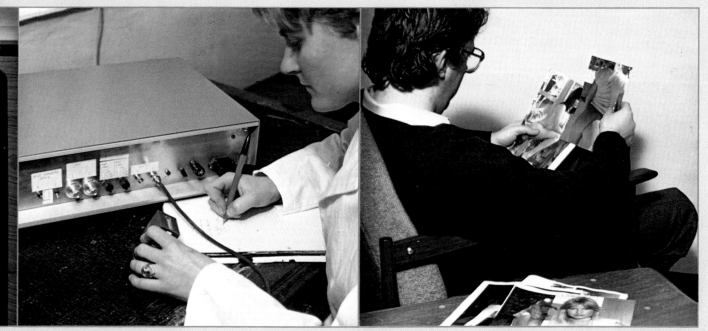

on no other hat. The next day, to her complete surprise, her daughter announced that she had just become engaged. Mrs Jones wore that hat to her daughter's wedding.

Some months later she was looking through her clothes cupboard when, for no apparent reason, her black skirt, which she had not worn for some time (and which was the only piece of black clothing she possessed), caught her eye. She decided to try it on to see if it still fitted and was pleased to see that it did. She tried on no other item of clothing. The next day news arrived of her mother's sudden death. Mrs Jones wore that black skirt to the funeral.

Even if these two incidents are coincidences they are particularly meaningful ones for Mrs Jones: her uncanny knack of encountering the appropriate clothes for the events of the immediate future is strikingly consistent with her everyday motivation to be appropriately dressed on every occasion.

Parapsychologists can now look at real life

A teacher's lawnmower refused to start every summer just when he had a stack of examination papers to mark – and his wife wanted him to mow the lawn. The paranormal nature of this 'coincidental' escape route became clear when the teacher discovered he was a metal bender. Judging by Stanford's research it seems that many people use PK or ESP, perhaps unknown to themselves, to bring about what they want

cases, deduce common themes underlying them, and then construct situations in the laboratory that allow them to be rigorously tested, and enable the odds against such 'coincidences' to be calculated statistically.

An example of this is the situation where you are faced with having to do a particular job that you really do not want to do and then, just before you begin it, something happens that frees you from the task. Many people must have had this experience and not given it a second thought.

A laboratory copy of this situation was set up using 40 male college students. They were given the following task, which was presented as a standard psychological experiment and which was deliberately made as boring as possible. They had to follow, with a light pen, the path of a randomly moving spot of light that was shown on a translucent screen, and try to predict the direction it

would take, using the light pen as a pointer. But meanwhile, unknown to them, a two-state random event generator (REG) was operating: equivalent to someone tossing a coin, the REG had an equal probability of registering one of two states. The REG was monitored by an experimental assistant who, if she noted seven consecutive occurrences of the same state, would release the subject of the experiment from his boring task and give him the job of sorting pictures of scantily clad women in order of attractiveness. None of the subjects knew before starting the task that there was any hope of escaping it, nor what reward their 'release' would bring; the only possible link between the subjects and the events generated by the REG was their subconscious mind. Of the 40 subjects, Stanford claimed, about three should have escaped by pure chance. In fact, eight did.

Lazy days of summer

This type of study indicates that ESP and PK can be jointly pressed into the service of individual desires. In my own research with people who can bend metal paranormally, many of them seem to use their PK abilities unconsciously to get what they want. One teacher in a Midlands technical college found that every summer, just as he began to be very busy marking examination papers and did not want to be distracted, his lawnmower would mysteriously refuse to start. His wife's pleas that he mow the lawn could therefore be justifiably refused on the grounds that the lawnmower was broken. In this case the PK-generated 'escape route' from the resented task was not suspected by the agent until he was discovered to be a metal bender and was asked if any domestic equipment had ever regularly malfunctioned in his vicinity. (The answer to this question has been found to be a useful indicator of hidden PK abilities.) Sometimes causing equipment to malfunction in this way can have very dramatic, even lifesaving, consequences:

A letter to the correspondence column of *The Sun* in the late 1970s related the story of a disabled driver of an invalid carriage. Normally reliable, the engine stalled for no apparent reason at a set of traffic lights while waiting for the green light. When the lights changed, the invalid carriage still refused to start, despite the driver's every effort. Then, a few seconds after the lights turned green, a heavy lorry shot through the red lights coming straight for where the invalid carriage would have been had its engine been functioning normally.

The 'mysterious' breakdown of machinery is arguably less mysterious if seen as a feature of the PMIR model – using PK to save oneself, even if one is not aware of it at the time. But one can learn to become aware of PMIR – and to reap the rewards.

Luck, judgement and psi

Do we make our own 'luck'? Do we use the subtlest influences of ESP to get what we want? This chapter explains the theory that claims that we can, and do, shape our everyday lives through psychic means

AMERICAN PARAPSYCHOLOGIST Rex G. Stanford formulated a theory – or, in the scientific jargon, a 'model' – that seeks to provide a framework within which the relationship between psi and everyday life can be examined. He gave this model the uncompromisingly academic title 'psi-mediated instrumental response', or PMIR (see page 1570), and he used it to explain how ordinary, 'non-psychic' people can bring about what they want through the subconscious use of ESP or psychokinesis (PK). But, assuming that the hidden use of psi is as widespread as Stanford claims, what is the mechanism behind it?

There seem to be several possible mechanisms involved; one of the commonest being implicit when a person instinctively alters his or her behaviour as a direct result of information received, more often than not subconsciously or subliminally, through ESP alone, even though this form of instant adjustment may appear to be no more than absent-minded deviations from a rigidly followed routine. Stanford quotes the following incident as an example:

A New Yorker was travelling by subway to pay a surprise visit to some friends living in another part of the city. At the 14th Street station he should have changed trains but

A correspondent of parapsychologist Rex G. Stanford met his Congressman – whom he had assumed was in Washington – in the New York subway at *precisely* the right moment to discuss urgent political issues with him. Stanford believes that such meetings are not accidental: we cause them to happen – but only when our need is at its most pressing

instead 'absent-mindedly' walked out into the street. Realising his mistake he decided to walk the six blocks to his friends' apartment. But as he was walking along he bumped into his friends, who were on their way to an appointment; nevertheless they were pleased to see him and chatted with him for some time. So he had actually made the 'right' move at the 14th Street station by walking out of it, even though it was 'wrong' in normal terms. If he had made the correct change at the station he would not have met his friends at all.

The same person also related another instance of everyday PMIR that highlights several more of its features. He had received a printed letter from his Congressman, Mr K, concerning the importance of several issues that were to be raised in the forthcoming session of Congress upon which Mr K would have to vote; Mr K requested suggestions, to be made on a tear-off form, as to how he should vote. Stanford's correspondent left the letter unanswered for some days, although he cared passionately about the issues raised. Then one night he decided to complete the form, and wrote a covering note, intending to give it to his secretary to post the next day. However, events overtook his intentions. The next morning he left for the office a little later than usual; he went to his customary subway station, arriving on the platform less than a minute before the incoming train. While he waited he felt a hand on his shoulder: he turned around – and there was his Congressman. They boarded the same train and spent the journey discussing the political issues that concerned them both. He had never met the Congressman in those circumstances before and has not since. And he had assumed that Mr K would at that time be in Washington rather than New York.

This story embodies several of the central points of the PMIR model; one is that the 'coincidental' meeting happened only when Stanford's correspondent felt an urgent need to discuss the political issues with his Congressman; and although all his actions were perfectly ordinary ones, the timing of his crucial 'mistake' was all-important. It is possible that both men had unconsciously co-ordinated their behaviour so that they met to mutual advantage.

Another example of changing the timing of routine behaviour by the use of ESP to one's own advantage concerns Joseph Friedman, a lecturer in parapsychology. He relates how he had been feeling increasingly annoyed by having to wait for long periods for a bus from his home in west London. Then one day he decided to do something about it, by deliberately using PMIR. This took the form of his waiting in his house until he felt the irresistible urge to rush out and catch the bus. He tried it – and he claims that the length of time he waited at the bus stop after that was dramatically reduced.

An unfair advantage?

This case was an example of fairly instant 'payoff' but everyone knows someone who spends most of his life waiting for his luck to change for the better. Stanford believes that PMIR is behind most so-called runs of 'luck' – both good and bad. Just as psychic means can be used, consciously or subconsciously, to bring about advantageous events, so they can also be used to one's own disadvantage – by someone who is basically self-destructive or riddled with guilt.

Parapsychological research seems, in fact, to be moving towards a confirmation of the power of positive thinking; since the 1970s American studies seem to have indicated that *visualising* PK increases the chances of it happening. But the determined pessimist, always literally envisaging the worst, is actually supplying his psyche with images that it accepts as goals, which it then actively works to bring about, inhibiting the achievement of positive results – perhaps independently of the conscious intentions and desires of the pessimist himself.

One of the most startling assumptions of the PMIR model is that very complex situations can be affected by PK. This is one of the most bizarre aspects of PK and operates in an entirely different way from our normal skills, which tend to decline sharply in effectiveness as the task becomes more complex.

But many examples of hidden PMIR in everyday life seem to come about fairly

Andy telephones his friend, author Julian Isaacs. They have discovered that whenever Isaacs has a strong need to talk to him, Andy feels an equally strong compulsion to call him on the telephone. Sometimes he even hears Isaacs calling 'Andy!' It seems that the very idea of calling someone often activates a latent telepathic link

simply. Stanford quotes a case where a couple who are strict vegetarians found themselves in an American city they had never visited before. They desperately wanted to eat at a vegetarian restaurant but had no idea where to find one. They stopped at a roadside diner; a group of people came in and sat at the next table – and proceeded to discuss the respective merits and exact whereabouts of several vegetarian restaurants in the city. Not only that, but they discussed Indian vegetarian restaurants, which serve a type of cuisine much prized by the couple and extremely rare in the United States. Presumably the PMIR here acted by influencing the group's decision about which roadside diner to visit.

In Britain some of the commonest PMIR experiences seem to involve the telephone.

Perhaps the *idea* of ringing someone tends to activate a telepathic link; often X telephones Y and discovers that Y's line is engaged – because, as it turns out, at that very moment Y is trying to telephone X. Another similar experience is where you think of contacting someone and then promptly bump into them 'by accident', or they telephone soon after you thought of them. This happened frequently to me in connection with one friend in particular, Andy, who lived some distance away and did not possess a telephone. Every time I had a real need to contact him he would telephone at that moment. Eventually this became so noticeable that I would deliberately try to make him telephone, 'telling' him to do so by ESP. It worked, demonstrating that the effect was no accident. In the end my friend would actually hear me shouting 'Andy!' The Irish have long recognised this telephone-PMIR, entitling it 'the bells', meaning that one hears

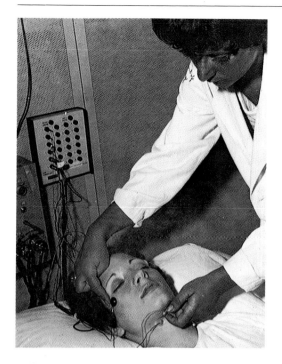

bells in one's head when someone is about to ring.

This raises the question of whether non-conscious ('non-intentional') PMIR can be made deliberate. Stanford proposes the theory that precognitive ESP, such as that involved in premonitions, is particularly likely to get through to our conscious mind because one of the functions of precognition may be to lessen the shock of the predicted event when it happens. Of course some types of precognition enable us to take avoiding action, and therefore the event never takes place. But some cases are unavoidable; we might have a premonition that involves someone else – a loved one suffering a heart attack, for example. Even if we knew, through ESP, that it was going to happen there is nothing we can do about it, but Stanford believes that the precognition serves as a buffer against the event.

Secrets of the sleeper

And of course dreams seem to be a very common outlet of unintentional ESP, although most people are not aware of it, either through poor dream recall or lack of interest. But participation in a dream group, where one is encouraged to recall and discuss one's dreams, rapidly reveals ESP at work. The classic studies of dream ESP at the Maimonides Center in New York have proved dream ESP to be widespread. But using one's psi deliberately is another matter; the mechanism behind it can perhaps be best understood by looking at what we know about factors that inhibit or prevent PMIR.

One of the essentials in encouraging PMIR is flexible behaviour. Often the potentially rewarding situation that one detects through ESP demands the sort of action to bring it about that is unusual or even bizarre. Sometimes absent-minded 'slips' – as in the case of

Above left: an experiment in dream research at the Maimonides Center in New York. Work there has shown ESP to be extremely common in dreams, even among people who do not consider themselves to be psychic. Does everyone therefore in some way use this dream ESP?

Right: Stanford's research points to a human, not a divine, source that effectively answers petitionary prayers. Controversially, he claims that earnest prayer activates one's own capacity for PK and it is this mechanism that 'answers' the prayer. Unanswered prayers might therefore be a case of one's own negative feelings inhibiting a positive result

the 'accidental' meeting with the Congress-man – can achieve the goal, but often it requires more than minimal deviation from normal behaviour and as such it can be achieved only by those who are prepared to act spontaneously. People with lives that are rigidly timetabled have fewer opportunities for PMIR. Many PMIR situations seem to happen to people on holiday, when their normal day-to-day routines are forgotten. But it does seem that an acceptance of the reality of psi and a readiness to recognise PMIR when it occurs are essential in order to encourage it to happen more often.

Stanford also examines the mechanism behind petitionary prayer and compares the psychological stance of the person who prays with that of the PK agent in laboratory work. He concludes that both PMIR and the answers to prayers are possibly the same thing, dressed up in different beliefs. They both work best when the need is greatest and when the subject does not consciously try to bring about the desired effect. In prayer, the

request for action is made to an apparently external agency – God, the saints, or the gods – who is believed to have the power to answer the prayer, with whatever action that might entail. Stanford controversially implies that human PK, and not divine intervention, may well be the agency that answers prayers. Of course if this is true then unanswered prayers can be explained as a direct result of harbour-ing negative or guilty feelings.

But even without attempting to control or direct one's spontaneous psi, the discovery of hidden PMIR adds a new dimension to every-day life. On investigation, PMIR reveals some surprisingly far-reaching and complex interactions in daily life, and the picture that emerges from Stanford's study is of human involvement with a much wider range of events in both time and space than we have hitherto suspected.

SORRAT

Psychokinetic effects are notoriously difficult to produce to order – a fact seized upon by sceptics. Yet the SORRAT group of Rolla, Missouri, have succeeded in causing a great variety of paranormal happenings.
JULIAN ISAACS tells their story

THE ENVELOPE MOVED on its own slowly and jerkily from behind the typewriter. It reached the flat top of the typewriter and slid slowly across it. Suddenly it tipped over onto the keyboard – and started to become transparent. Then it vanished completely. This astonishing evidence of psychokinesis (PK) and teleportation was a highlight of one of the most extraordinary 'home movie' shows ever and, not unnaturally, those present asked their host to re-run that particular film. There had been 10 fairly primitive films shown, all shot on standard 8-millimetre film and all showing a wide range of psychokinetic – mind over matter – effects. And nearly all of them had been filmed inside a locked glass box to which only one person, the experimenter himself, their host for the

Minds over matter

evening, had the key.

In the weeks that followed, the implications of that evening's 'home movie' session slowly became apparent. If the film had shown genuinely paranormal events – and there was no evidence to prove otherwise – and if they could be reproduced by other groups elsewhere, then parapsychology was on the brink of an enormously significant breakthrough. If PK could be filmed, especially in its more exotic and rare forms, then it could be submitted to detailed study and perhaps give scientists the long-awaited foothold on understanding the elusive

physics of psychical phenomena.

Those films shown on a November evening in 1980 in Rolla, Missouri, USA, were the culmination of a long project that had begun in October 1961 with the formation of the Society for Research into Rapport and Telekinesis (SORRAT). This group is probably the USA's most successful producer of long-term, large-scale PK (called 'macro-PK' by parapsychologists).

SORRAT was founded by John G. Neihardt, professor of English literature at the University of Missouri at Columbia. A powerful, charismatic personality and a man of wide interests, he had been fascinated by the paranormal for many years. He was intrigued by the way those people with strong spiritualist beliefs or with a mystical background seemed to attract PK. Neihardt himself was a close friend of the Sioux Indian holy man Black Elk, and as a result was made an honorary member of the Oglala Sioux tribe. Some of the former members of SORRAT believe that he was actually initiated as a Sioux shaman (magician and holy man) and there are even rumours that Neihardt himself handed on this secret initiation to one of the SORRAT members.

This kind of belief may have helped the SORRAT group achieve their remarkable evidence of macro-PK; certainly some of its members were known to possess outstanding psychic gifts. The group, meeting every Friday night at Professor Neihardt's home,

Top, above and right: Dr J. T. Richards (in the striped shirt) and members of SORRAT make a light metal table rise into the air – levitated, they believe, by 'spirits'

Left: the late Professor John G. Neihardt, founder of the SORRAT group. It was rumoured that he was initiated as a Sioux shaman by his close friend, Black Elk; this magical background may have helped him to create the atmosphere of belief that apparently encourages paranormal phenomena

Right: Joseph Mangini, said to be possessed by the spirit of Black Elk during a SORRAT meeting. He is holding a *wichasha wakon*, or holy staff, and embracing Professor Neihardt's daughter Alice

Below right: a hat is levitated a few inches from a desk top

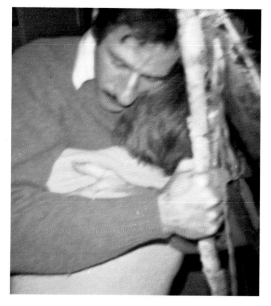

registered a drop of up to 5° in the normal room temperature. And a few months later paranormal rapping began.

These paranormal raps were crucial to the later success of the group mainly because they provided an enormous boost to its confidence and paved the way for other, more complicated, phenomena. But first the group began testing the circumstances surrounding the rapping. For example, raps were still heard when everyone in the group lay down so that their hands and feet were clearly in sight. The raps even occurred outdoors, apparently coming from underground. Indoors they would obligingly move around the room on request, the group sitting quite still meanwhile. And significantly, the raps displayed intelligence, using codes with which to answer questions, even on some later occasions conveying information that was unknown to any member who

Skyrim Farm, Missouri, grew very close over the 16 years they were together. Originally there were 30 members, but the 'regulars' consisted of 15 to 20 of the more strongly motivated.

The techniques used by SORRAT to induce psychokinetic events were similar to those used by many Spiritualist development circles. Essentially they simply sat around in a group in a carefree and light-hearted manner while waiting for PK to occur. One member of the group, Mr Joseph Mangini, developed the ability to go into a trance – and then PK phenomena were often particularly strong. After meetings had continued for only two months it was found that areas of seemingly paranormal coldness would develop around small target objects laid out on a table top. Thermometers placed near these objects

was present. So the raps, simple or complex, provided audible evidence that the group was getting somewhere and they created a sense of expectancy and excitement. What would happen next?

Apart from the positive psychological effects, the raps also served a practical purpose. They opened up a two-way channel of communication between whatever was causing them (called 'the agency' – a deliberately neutral term chosen by William E. Cox, later the group's scientific collaborator) and the group itself. The group used the raps as a code, 'agreeing' with the agency that one, two or three raps would mean 'yes', 'no', and 'maybe' respectively. In this way the group held simple question and answer sessions. The agency could also deliver messages using an alphabetic code – one rap for A, two for B and so on. Once established, this was then used by the group to ask the agency to perform certain PK tasks, which could then be graded.

Groups who aim to achieve macro-PK need to increase the level of difficulty of the tasks they set the agency only gradually – in

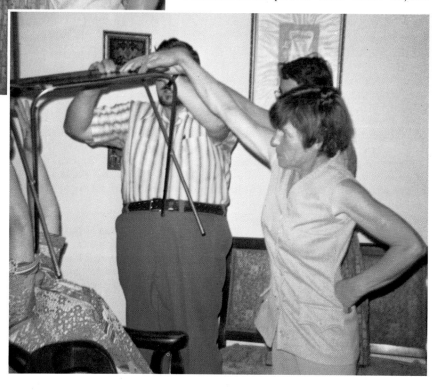

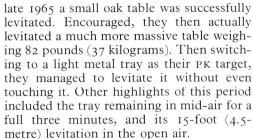

The SORRAT 'spirits' produced a spectacular variety of PK phenomena, which began with paranormal rapping and went on to include a host of levitations (above right and far right) and a 'walking' table (above and right). On another occasion the group managed to levitate a table without touching it (below), and once a tray rose unaided 15 feet (4.5 metres) into the air. The 'Philip' group of Toronto also had a 'walking' table – a star attraction of the Canadian television programme made about Philip – which climbed the steps to the platform on which the group were sitting

late 1965 a small oak table was successfully levitated. Encouraged, they then actually levitated a much more massive table weighing 82 pounds (37 kilograms). Then switching to a light metal tray as their PK target, they managed to levitate it without even touching it. Other highlights of this period included the tray remaining in mid-air for a full three minutes, and its 15-foot (4.5-metre) levitation in the open air.

The SORRAT scrapbooks, kept by Dr J. T. Richards, the group's archivist and photographer, contain many photographs of a host of other objects being affected by psychokinetic forces. And apart from PK, the group induced other psychic phenomena that were, as far as possible, recorded by Dr Richards – such as mysterious lights, apports, teleportation of objects and, on one celebrated occasion, the appearance of a remarkably life-like full-form apparition on the lawn (which obligingly waited to be photographed). Dr Richards modestly estimates that only one in three of SORRAT's attempts to create PK effects succeeded fully, but these successes were often spectacular compared to the weak PK usually achieved in laboratory experiments.

For many years Professor Neihardt had kept in touch with Dr J. B. Rhine (regarded by some as the father of modern parapsychology) and naturally Dr Rhine was fascinated by the reports of SORRAT's phenomenal successes. Rhine enlisted the help of

this way they are less likely to fail. And SORRAT found one of the advantages of communication with the agency was that it could refuse to do a task it considered too hard. In this way the number of tasks failed was small, helping to maintain a positive interest in the group. Another advantage of communicating with the PK agency was that the group could give it orders, which were obeyed, proving that it was the group, not the agency, that was in control.

One of the most important aspects of the raps was that the agency causing them claimed to consist of a group of spirits. This interpretation was readily accepted by many members of SORRAT who were Spiritualists. From the experimenters' points of view this was a great advantage because these people did not feel personally responsible for trying to make anything happen. And conscious effort – straining to make PK occur – has been proved many times, especially in paranormal metal bending, to be counter-productive, apparently actually preventing it happening.

But the identity of the PK agency remained unclear because, although parapsychologists tend to adopt the humanistic viewpoint – preferring to believe that psychical effects are due to the living rather than the dead – the SORRAT 'spirits' later made rather eloquent and striking claims for their independent existence (see page 18). The group's PK effects gradually became so strong that by

his laboratory's PK specialist William Cox, who, apart from being an original and inventive experimenter, also happened to be an experienced stage magician. Rhine believed he would be invaluable in developing some kind of fraud-proof device inside which SORRAT's PK could be encouraged to take place. A locked box of some sort seemed the obvious answer – in other words a miniature PK laboratory, or minilab.

The prototype minilab, constructed by Professor Neihardt, was a huge glass container, but effects in it were very rare and limited. Cox adapted the idea, making smaller versions out of shallow wooden boxes, which were later called coffee boxes because in the experiments a layer of dried coffee grounds would usually be spread on

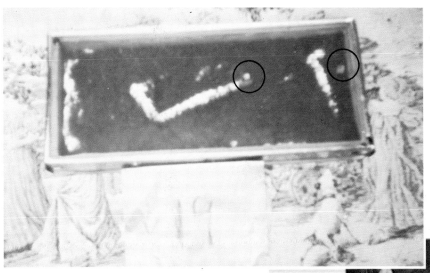

Other boxes had no coffee grounds and were equipped with a sheet of carbon paper and a stylus. The agency caused the stylus to write by itself – by pressing down on the carbon paper and leaving scrawls on the white floor. 'Direct writing' (as writing by PK alone became known) resulted in various sorts of communications: sometimes mere scrawls, sometimes whole words, would be written – forerunners of the much more elaborate and coherent messages left in the later minilabs (see page 18).

In 1977 Cox retired from Rhine's laboratory and devoted himself to the intensive study of the SORRAT PK. He took the opportunity to test the coffee boxes while actually

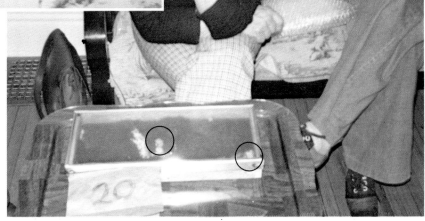

the box floor. The joints of each box and the seal on its glass lid were constructed in such a way that the box could not be opened without the special markers that had been incorporated into the joints when they were made.

A broken trail

For the experiments, a variety of objects would be placed in the box, and a layer of coffee grounds would be spread on the box floor. Then the agency would be set a specific task. For example, one task consisted of moving one of a pair of dice through the coffee grounds, while leaving the other where it was. The task was specifically devised to prevent the effects being achieved simply by the box tilting – deliberately or accidentally – which would have made both dice move. This particular test was often successful, sometimes providing the added bonus of the moving die leaving a broken trail, as if it had hopped across the coffee grounds. The only conclusion was that the die had actually levitated from place to place.

Sometimes only coffee grounds were placed in the box, and the agency was given the task of producing visible trails in the grounds, exposing the white floor of the box.

Top and above: dice (ringed), moved only by PK, plough a path through a layer of coffee grounds on the floor of a shallow box, exposing the light-coloured timber beneath. Other dice trails were broken – as if the dice had hopped

Below: while in a trance, SORRAT member Joseph Mangini lightly touches a table as it 'walks' up the wall

at Skyrim, and made the momentous discovery that PK effects would occur spontaneously, while no one was trying to produce them or, as far as anyone knew, even thinking about them. This totally disproved the common idea that PK requires massive concentration and effort. And the fact that the coffee boxes could be left alone and *still produce PK* was to be exploited in later minilab experiments with astonishing results. It is the phenomenon of spontaneous PK more than anything else that makes the work of the SORRAT group so important.

This preliminary research convinced Cox that SORRAT's effects were genuine. But with the death of Professor Neihardt in 1973 the group began to lose its impetus. However, two SORRAT members, Joseph Mangini and Dr Richards, had already begun to experience spontaneous PK of various sorts as individuals.

Cox settled in Rolla specifically to study PK in the Richards's home. The results of this collaboration have provoked amazement and disbelief among many professional parapsychologists for whom they are simply too good to be true. But despite the criticism and incredulity, the paranormal events at Dr Richards's home were soon to become too astonishing to be ignored.

A pen levitates and writes by itself, leather rings link and unlink, and strange poems suddenly appear – these are only some of the psychokinetic effects in the SORRAT group's minilab.

THE SORRAT GROUP'S outstanding success in inducing psychokinesis (PK) led parapsychologist William E. Cox to install a minilab at their headquarters at Skyrim Farm, Missouri, USA, in the summer of 1977. The first successful minilab consisted of a perspex box of about one cubic foot (0.03 cubic metres) volume, which was secured to a stout wooden base by steel strips and two padlocks. Cox put various 'toys' inside it for the PK agency to play with. Several minor PK effects happened while the box was at Skyrim Farm, the most outstanding of which was the apparently paranormal arrival of pieces of old Indian beaded leather inside the securely

Cox and box

locked and sealed perspex minilab.

The first minilab was then transferred to the home of Dr J. T. Richards in Rolla, Missouri, where Cox also lived. Dr Richards had the double distinction of being both SORRAT's historian and a focus for considerable PK activity, especially paranormal rapping – although he chose to explain it as the work of spirits, rather than of his own subconscious. Various types of PK phenomena took place in the first minilab, and perhaps the most intriguing happened when Cox was present. On this occasion the minilab contained clean paper, a pencil, dried peas dyed white and blue, a small glass, leather rings firmly attached to a point inside the box, a set of six spools strung on a wire with twisted ends, and miscellaneous other small objects.

Several friends of Dr Richards who were interested in psychic matters had met at his house and gathered around the minilab, which was on a coffee table in the sitting room. They turned out the light and waited. Suddenly they heard noises from inside the box; PK activity was taking place. Cox was telephoned and he arrived at the farm in time to hear what he construed as the dried peas jumping about inside the minilab. Then there was silence and the light was turned on again. On investigation, the group discovered that the locks were still secure, but some surprising changes had taken place inside the box. One of the six spools was missing and the ring of wire on which they had been strung had had its ends re-twisted differently. Thirty blue peas had apparently

Above: the locked and sealed minilab in the basement of Dr J. T. Richards's home in Rolla, Missouri. A die has moved – apparently of its own volition – leaving a white trail where it has ploughed through a layer of coffee grounds on the floor of the minilab, exposing the white wood beneath. An unidentified white object has also levitated above the raised tin in the centre

Left: consecutive frames from one of the Rolla 'home movies' showing the paranormal linking of two seamless leather rings outside the minilab

Far right: a white envelope moves smoothly out of its outer envelope – which *remains sealed*

Below: W. E. Cox with some metal objects that bent while secured in the minilab. The aluminium bar, which is $\frac{1}{2}$ inch (1.2 centimetres) thick, was bent 11°. The round white object is what remained of a plastic thermometer after it partially melted while in the minilab. The spoon bent after being sealed in the minilab by a locksmith – who swore that the lock remained secure

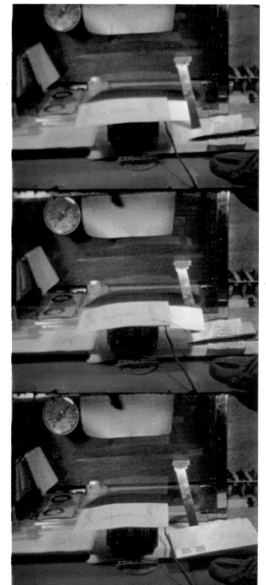

therefore fraudulent. But reports of telekinesis and teleportation have a long history and have persistently cropped up in the literature of psychical research; for example there are accounts of well-witnessed teleportation in Professor John Hasted's *Metal-benders* (1981). Viewed from an historical perspective Cox's results are by no means unique, although the fact that they are recorded on film adds to their significance.

Cox's second and third minilabs were set up in a small room in the basement of Dr Richards's home in Rolla. They were fish tanks turned upside down onto a thick wooden board. They differed only in that the third was larger than the second and in minor details regarding the position of the locks. A strip of steel was wrapped tightly round each minilab, then passed through two slits in the baseboard and under the base. The ends of the band were secured together by a high-quality padlock. The minilabs were then locked onto their baseboards and the narrow slit between each tank and its board was sealed with a rubber gasket; this effectively

jumped into the glass, two straight pipe-cleaners were now twisted into linked rings and the leather rings had been dislodged.

Shortly before this, Cox met a Mr S.C. who rapidly became a valued collaborator; he suggested and helped to set up ciné camera facilities so that any PK inside the second and third minilabs could be filmed while it was happening. Target objects for PK action were linked to special switches so that whenever an object moved the switch was triggered. The switches were wired to a timing device that in turn automatically switched on two lights and triggered a ciné camera to shoot a 30-second sequence of film showing whatever was happening inside the locked minilab. A 12-hour clock was also set in front of the camera so the timing of any PK activity would be shown (the later British minilabs use 24-hour clocks that also show the date, thus pinpointing the events precisely). This is how all later film of PK activity in minilabs has been shot. Cox's first set-up was crude – the ciné camera was clockwork so it sometimes ran down, the lights were not very powerful so that definition was poor and the standard 8-millimetre film added to the problems of obtaining good quality pictures. The timer was also triggered falsely on several occasions.

Sceptics will, in view of the extraordinary nature of the events filmed at Rolla, simply write off all minilab PK as 'impossible' and

Above: this sealed bottle acted as a kind of 'minilab'. Various objects were placed in it: a couple of pipecleaners, a pencil stub, a piece of paper and a safety pin. Acted upon by PK the pipecleaners became the 'man' who wrote 'Freedom, love, faith' on the paper with the pencil stub

stopped anyone being able to slip anything through the gap. To improve security further, Cox used some special plastic string, obtainable only from Germany, which he tied tightly round the ends of the steel strip; the ends of the string were then melted together and bound with adhesive tape. Lastly, Cox impressed the insignia of his notary's ring into the melted plastic while it was still warm. Cox had sole charge of the two keys to each padlock and had complete control over how the objects were set up inside the minilabs.

So if one wanted to assume that the minilab PK events were fraudulent two questions would have to be asked: who is doing the cheating – and how? Given Cox's background of more than 30 years' PK research and a few years' successful work with minilabs it seems most unlikely that he would have failed to detect any fraud perpetrated by others in the group. Cox's record also speaks powerfully against his being in collusion with others; in 30 years in J.B. Rhine's laboratory there was never any occasion to doubt his honesty and integrity.

A box of tricks?

Shifting their ground, sceptics might then point out that the objects inside the minilabs could easily be manipulated with fine threads, but judging by the evidence of all film shot at Rolla it becomes obvious that the activity in the minilabs was far too complex and co-ordinated to be produced in that way. Another accusation is that the films were animated. Animation would involve taking a series of single frame shots of the minilab and its contents, the objects being moved very small distances between each shot – so that when the film is shown at the normal speed of 18 frames per second the objects appear to be moving on their own and continuously. This would be an enormously time-consuming task and a dummy minilab would have to be set up secretly to avoid detection, for the real minilab is frequently visited and is in a busy domestic environment. Of course it is possible to maintain the fraud hypothesis by assuming that everybody concerned was in collusion, or that Cox and Richards have a secret film studio somewhere. But once other groups of researchers start to reproduce the Rolla results the fraud hypothesis will become increasingly less tenable.

The first filmed events were obtained in May 1979 and showed a levitating pen. Shortly afterwards further sequences were filmed of this pen engaged in 'direct writing' inside the locked and sealed minilab. Among the words written the name 'John King' was prominent – King being the control claimed by several mediums, notably the Italian Eusapia Palladino, and 'he' figures as one of the group of ostensible spirits associated with minilab experiments. On 4 July 1979 a pen was filmed writing the words 'Glorious Fourth' on some paper outside of, and in

Part One (abbreviated) of a 1,900-word Notarized Deposition from Mr. R. Henson of Abel Lock & Key, Rolla, Missouri:

County of Phelps

City of Rolla, Mo.

I have been asked to examine an aquarium tank by Mr. W. E. Cox of this city, and the security of its attachment to a solid wooden base...

...I have inserted my own lock into the hasp, and have permanently plugged it... If serious alterations of the objects in it later occur, I am quite willing to testify to it in the presence of a public notary, since I do not believe this is in fact possible without first destroying my lock. Its keyway I chose also to seal with superglue and then tape.

Signed: *[signature]* Witnessed: *[signature]* 5/8/81

Part Two (abbreviated):

At my shop on May 12, 1981, Mr. Cox brought to me the same container...I could not find any evidence that the plugged and permanently-glued Master Lock had been opened, nor had the sealed paper cover over the keyway (bearing my imprint) been punctured or torn...

...We could see that various changes had now occurred inside... I certainly cannot understand how these things have taken place...

Signed: *[signature]*
ABEL LOCK & KEY
117 So. Bishop A—
Rolla, Mo. 65401

Witnessed: *[signature]*
" (W. E. Cox)

[signature] , a Notary Public, do certify that Mr. Ronnie Henson and Mr. W. E. Cox appeared before me on May 14, 1981, and that Mr. Henson has declared that both Part One and Part Two of this document to which my signature is affixed is true and correct in every particular.

5/14/81 *[signature]* my com. exp. 6-29

front of, the minilab. As with much of the direct writing, the motion of the pen was extraordinarily rapid – Cox estimates a writing speed of more than double his own. A slower example of PK from this early period is that of an aluminium film canister 'walking' inside the locked minilab. It can be seen slowly edging its way across the width of the tank, stumbling a little over a minor obstruction near the middle.

It was in May 1979 that Cox unexpectedly obtained hard evidence of teleportation connected with the minilab. On the floor of the basement he found a green felt-tipped pen that he knew he had safely locked inside the minilab the night before.

Comings and goings

The tally of teleportation events is now a long one. Pipecleaners, water, matchbooks, peas, pens, delicate mica sheets, string, small toys, jewellery, film, metal objects, and paper have all passed into or out of minilabs.

A classic experiment in this area is the paranormal linking of two rings. Cox has obtained more than six of these events on film, the first in the summer of 1979. The film clearly reveals that the rings are indeed interlinked – but only for a brief period before they separate again. The actual interlinkage happens between frames so no pictures exist of the 'halfway' situation. Irritatingly, the rings (made of several grades of

Above: the abbreviated form of a deposition signed by a Rolla locksmith who declared that the lock he fitted to 'an aquarium tank . . . with a solid wooden base' (the minilab) was not tampered with in any way, yet 'various changes have occurred inside' and he 'certainly cannot see how these things have taken place'. However, security was only gradually imposed after PK was achieved reasonably frequently; an experiment that is over-secure in the early stages often has the effect of discouraging PK completely

leather) have always unlinked again so that no permanent linkages have been left as evidence. In their written messages to the alleged spirits co-operating in the minilab research Cox and Richards have laid much stress on the importance of permanent linkages. Amusingly, one of the 'spirits' replied: 'We've tried, but we can't make the damn leather rings stay linked – sorry. John King.'

The variety and frequency of minilab PK have continued to grow, and later events filmed in the locked and sealed minilab have included the sorting of dyed peas into single-colour groups, the sorting of cards into suits and the blowing up of balloons. Paranormal metal bending has taken place inside the minilabs; spontaneous combustion has also occurred, and the variety of telekinetic actions recorded is extremely wide.

The freedom with which material objects have apparently passed through the minilab walls has led the Rolla group to use it as a paranormal 'postbox'. The disappearance of letters has been filmed and a few days later these letters have been delivered through the normal postal service. As this 'PK post' practice grew, the envelopes were left open in the minilab and a motley selection of objects surrounding them would be telekinetically popped inside before the letters were teleported. It was noticed very often that foreign stamps would somehow find their way on to the envelopes so that the letters would arrive bearing dated Australian, Italian or South

Many of the classic phenomena repeatedly described in the literature of psychical research have also been reported as happening in the minilab. These include the abrupt and mysterious appearance (an 'apport' in Spiritualist terms) of a piece of typing and direct writing (left); the swift levitation of two leather rings (above) and the spontaneous combustion of a piece of paper on the floor of the box (above right). On another occasion the glass at the top right hand side of the minilab cracked – when a candle inside spontaneously ignited. If these and other reported examples of minilab PK are authentic then they represent a breakthrough in PK experimentation

American stamps. The PK takes the path of least resistance since the postmarks invariably read 'Rolla' and the letters seem to spend little time between disappearing from the minilab and arriving at the Rolla sorting office. In the UK Dr John Beloff and the author have received several of these letters.

One of the exciting potentialities of minilab research for the future is the teleportation of small devices containing electronic sensors and radio transmitters or some very compact form of cassette recorder. Using 'space probes' of this sort might allow physicists to obtain information about what happens to objects when they disappear.

Meanwhile, perhaps the last word should be left to those immaterial minilab jokers. The following verse is one of several that have appeared in the basement at Rolla. This specimen was typed, apparently paranormally, on a typewriter deliberately supplied with paper and left outside the minilab, but similar offerings have been produced within it. It is certainly a fitting tribute to the pioneer of minilab research:

A clever man, W.E. Cox,
Made a really remarkable box;
In it, we, with PK,
In the usual way,
Wrote, spite of bands, seals and locks!

Lights...cameras...action!

Claims for PK in the American minilabs have met with severe criticism but, as we see in this chapter, the British minilab programme is designed to provide positive proof for or against the phenomenon

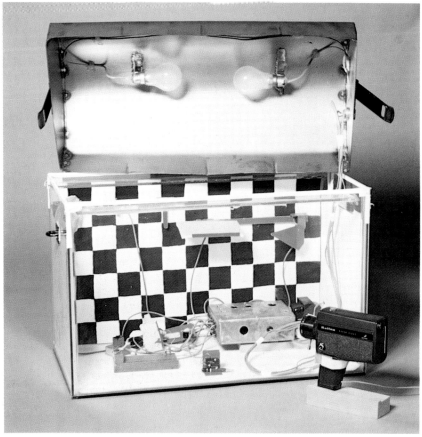

concept of teleportation that the phenomenon tends to be acknowledged. And for the less psychic the chances of recognising it are even slimmer.

After seeing the SORRAT film and discussing the events filmed with W.E. Cox and Dr J.T. Richards the author set out to achieve similar effects – but much faster – by choosing his subjects carefully. The British minilab programme began, therefore, with a series of three lectures given to a selected audience in the English Midlands in May 1980. It consisted entirely of convinced Spiritualists. They were to be screened as potential minilab agents because they already accept the existence of psi, are often psychically gifted and practised – and they are more likely to experience and recognise teleportation than others.

Spectacular stories

The Spiritualists were also shown some of the SORRAT ciné film to interest them in the programme and perhaps to stimulate some memories of 'background PK' they might have experienced but dismissed at the time. Then they were asked if they had any personal experience of teleportation. The harvest of stories was quite spectacular.

Although an indeterminate number of reported teleportation events can be ascribed to faulty memory, misperception (not seeing something that is there), absentmindedness and so on, these people related stories that were backed with so much circumstantial evidence that it was difficult to categorise them as other than truthful accounts – or

THE AMAZING PK effects produced in the first American minilabs were the result of 16 years' regular meetings of the SORRAT group, but when the British minilab programme began in 1980 it was hoped to obtain PK almost immediately. The idea was to use subjects who had already experienced PK in their lives *before* taking part in the experiment.

The author based the programme on an assumption that seems, at first sight, startling to say the least. This was that at least some people were experiencing teleportation (the paranormal disappearance and reappearance of objects) sporadically and spontaneously in their everyday lives. This form of 'domestic PK' (paranormal happenings in the home) often goes unnoticed or is discounted because it is 'impossible'. Even gifted psychics usually tend to ignore odd disappearances or reappearances as 'silly' and meaningless because there is no rational explanation for them. It is only if events become overwhelming (such as in poltergeist cases) or if the person experiencing them is familiar with the

Left: the first British minilab, designed and built by Julian Isaacs at Aston University, Birmingham. The chequerboard pattern is to facilitate the computation of the speed of objects that move by PK alone. The red bar supports two arms that hold letters. If a letter levitates, an arm rises, releasing a microswitch, which activates the lights and camera – resulting in 30 seconds of filmed PK. One of the arms has been bent by PK

Below left: some of the 'toys' donated for the minilab's PK agent to act on

Top: a brass spoon mounted so that, should it bend, it would make contact with the silver wire. It did bend, but only after the minilab became non-functional owing to an electrical fault

Above: two yellow-painted aluminium strips, mounted in a U shape so that they each press down a microswitch. If they bent through PK, they would release their microswitches and instantly initiate filming. They bent and actually intertwined – but irritatingly the event was not filmed because of an electrical malfunction in the minilab

deliberate lies. For instance, the teleported object may have gone missing very shortly after being put in a specific place, too soon to have been forgotten, and when found would be in a different and very obvious place. Members of the audience who reported instances of teleportation were then invited to a fourth lecture to which non-Spiritualist psychics were also invited. This combined audience was requested to swap teleportation stories and was encouraged to attempt some preparatory minilab experiments at home.

The rationale behind the 'telling a yarn' procedure is that PK tends to be highly responsive to suggestion. Even talking about paranormal happenings is a potent way of encouraging them to happen. And as the SORRAT group proved, maintaining interest is the key to obtaining striking results.

At this stage no one can tell whether the agents actually need to be members of PK groups before producing PK in the minilab at home. Unfortunately some PK groups do not manage to maintain the optimistic and positive approach needed to be successful and

therefore the individual members may never have a chance of developing as agents. However, the British programme represents a step into the unknown and it may be that a pattern emerges upon which future minilab research can be based.

The American minilab project possesses two great advantages in encouraging PK. One is the presence of an interested and concerned investigator, William E. Cox, who has been assiduous in attending his minilab and in maintaining the high level of interest in the group. The other advantage is that, although instances of PK in the Rolla minilab are not witnessed as they happen, they are automatically filmed (see page 14). This means that the effects can be seen by a wider audience than just the SORRAT group and wherever they are seen they inspire new people with an interest in the subject. There may well be a snowball effect whereby the film sparks off enough motivation in the viewers that there will be a rapid rise in the generation of PK.

In the British project, the preparatory minilab experiments, which are very simple and non-technical, are described on a set of information sheets; these are given to anyone who reports frequent teleportation and who is interested in controlling the phenomenon. Target objects – preferably ones that have been acted upon by PK before – are put in specific places and a written log is kept recording their movements, including any disappearances and reappearances; this effectively sidesteps faulty memory. The objects are checked every few days.

The next step involves the use of two shoeboxes as 'coffee boxes' (see page 14). A thin layer of coffee grounds or used tea leaves is spread upon the bottom of each box and a variety of small objects – such as marbles or small ornaments – are put in the box. The shoeboxes are then labelled on the lid and the base and put where they are unlikely to be disturbed (except by PK). A record is kept of which items are in the box and their position. The boxes and their contents are inspected every few days. The objects may move around inside the boxes or may even teleport from one box to the other.

If PK does start to happen more varied PK tasks are set. But the important thing at this early stage is to forget about security, the guiding principle being to concentrate on obtaining the PK first and only employing secure conditions once the phenomena start to happen reasonably often. The experimenter takes care to keep in touch with the subjects and when the frequency and extent of PK is satisfactory a fully equipped minilab is substituted for the shoeboxes. Even so, full

security is applied only once a number of ostensibly paranormal events have been filmed inside the unlocked minilab.

But what causes the PK to happen? Although there are no straight answers the experimenter suggests that Spiritualists, or any others to whom the idea appeals, make contact with any spirits they believe will help and ask them to assist the minilab programme by causing PK. Requests for specific PK effects can be written down and the messages left near the target objects as they were at Rolla, along with pens, pencils and paper for any 'direct writing' replies. But if the idea of 'spirits' is too implausible appeals can be made in the same way to one's own subconscious, for it is generally accepted by parapsychologists that the subconscious often acts separately from the conscious mind. But if the subconscious is invoked it must be addressed as if it were a separate entity, for it will act only if kept dissociated from one's consciousness.

By mid 1980 the first British minilab was

Above: the second British minilab, which was built almost exclusively for detecting paranormal metal bending, although it was also fitted with two leather rings hanging from supports that were connected to microswitches. The metal objects were set up so that if they bent they would touch the bare wires arranged round them, which would in turn trigger off the lights and camera (not seen here). The matt black background makes it easier to see any movement of the metal objects. By late 1981 the most successful examples of British minilab PK were of paranormal metal bending

Left: a Spiritualist couple from Coventry, England, with a brass ornament that they believed to have teleported while they attended one of Julian Isaacs's lectures

Right: 'Peter' with some of his bent metal. He is one of the very few paranormal metal benders who is also a poltergeist focus (another is Matthew Manning). The substantial metal bar he is holding in his left hand bent during a 30-minute period of meditation, while his sister remained in the same room. The bar proved too strong for the author to bend manually

in the home of 'Peter', a former poltergeist focus, in the Midlands. His exuberant and spontaneous PK had started after he discovered his very powerful metal bending ability. Besides this, Peter has apparently generated a large number of telekinetic and teleportation events including the teleportation of £25 in notes, which were put into an envelope that was folded in half and then taped many times all over the sides and joins. It was treated in this way because the wad of money had already disappeared and reappeared several times. The taped envelope was put into the zipped compartment of his mother's purse, which she carried in her pocket. She suddenly felt the purse go flat. On inspection the envelope was found to be taped exactly as before – but all the money was missing.

Left: a note pad bearing a message in 'direct writing'. It reads, 'Hi, fooled ya, it ain't pluged (*sic*) in' and is signed 'Quazer' – one of the other-dimensional 'super heroes' chosen by Peter, a Marvel Comic fan, to help him produce minilab PK. The message refers to the fact that the minilab that had been installed in Peter's home was set up, but not plugged in, nor was the lid secured. The pencil in the holder depresses a microswitch; if the pencil moved it would trigger the switch, which would activate the lights and camera

rapidly to have been found. But it does suggest that devices that transmit both radio waves and sound (perhaps ultrasonic sound) would be worthwhile trying to teleport in case it is still possible to keep track of them by sound alone when they are invisible. So possibly the calculator story has opened up important new lines of investigation.

Peter has achieved a limited success with his minilab. Although by late 1981 his powers had declined, he did generate some authentically paranormal metal bending inside the minilab and the tank itself was seen shaking and moving from place to place.

Other minilabs were, by late 1981, being equipped to be set up in the homes of potential agents. And the search for PK 'stars' goes on.

It may be that the work of the SORRAT group proves to be a turning point in parapsychology; certainly it has inspired a major PK programme in Britain, which may produce far-reaching results.

Peter also claims to have been teleported bodily from place to place more than once. There is some supporting evidence for this but unfortunately none of the occasions was adequately witnessed. But there are several accounts of people being teleported in the literature of psychical research – Mrs Samuel Guppy's apparently paranormal transportation across London in her nightclothes for example, or Uri Geller's sudden shocked arrival at Ossining, New York, from New York City, as alleged by investigator Dr Andrija Puharich. There are also reports of animals being teleported without harm.

Musical chairs

But one teleportation event did happen in Peter's presence that was witnessed and is of potentially great significance. Peter and his sister were sitting in the lounge of their parents' home when an electronic calculator – the kind that plays a series of notes held in its memory – vanished from under a pile of papers and magazines: the calculator's tune was suddenly heard, apparently coming from under a chair. They immediately tipped the chair up and checked underneath but no calculator was to be seen. However a few minutes later the tune was heard again, this time coming from under the settee. Peter and his sister looked under it but there was nothing there. This sequence happened several times, with the invisible calculator apparently moving about under the various pieces of furniture in the room, playing its tune. There is no reason to doubt the sister's word, for in all other incidents her testimony has proved to be impeccable.

This story presents us with the intriguing idea that objects might become invisible while they are still audible. Of course this is by no means the only paranormal explanation for the calculator story – it may, for example, have moved from place to place too

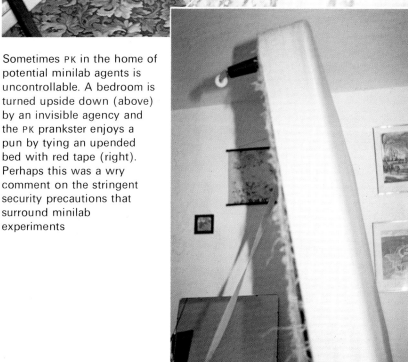

Sometimes PK in the home of potential minilab agents is uncontrollable. A bedroom is turned upside down (above) by an invisible agency and the PK prankster enjoys a pun by tying an upended bed with red tape (right). Perhaps this was a wry comment on the stringent security precautions that surround minilab experiments

Paranormal phenomena tend not to happen in laboratories; therefore, said the scientific establishment, they never happen at all. Why then, asks DAVID HARVEY, are more and more scientists keen to investigate the world of parapsychology?

The Cinderella science

OF ALL THE SCIENCES, that of parapsychology has the most far-reaching implications for Man. Yet, since its beginnings in the 1930s, it has met with bitter opposition, intolerance and hostility from other scientists – so much so that parapsychology is barely recognised as a legitimate academic discipline, and those few brave scientists who seek to study it have either to approach it through an accepted field of study – such as psychology – or pursue it as a sideline, through such organisations as the Society for Psychical Research (SPR).

Why is this? For parapsychology (which means 'beyond psychology') is the study of psychic phenomena – such as psychokinesis (PK), poltergeist phenomena, ESP and dream telepathy – among other unexplained abilities of the human mind. And such happenings, history assures us, have been observed for thousands of years.

All too often, however, strange phenomena have been associated with demons, angels or fairies, and have accumulated a combination of religious, superstitious and occult connotations. Even today parapsychology is frequently shunned because of an 'occult' tag and is bracketed with the activities of the deluded and the deranged.

Before J. B. Rhine began his pioneering

laboratory work into the search for 'psi' – or the unknown force behind psychic phenomena – in the 1930s, parapsychology was known as 'psychical research'. It was the province of enthusiastic members of the leisured classes, such as Sir William Crookes and Sir Arthur Conan Doyle, and revolved mainly around the investigation of mediums and the quest for proof of the afterlife.

Rhine, however, was more interested in phenomena that are demonstrably products of the human brain (such as ESP) and concentrated on examining these effects in the laboratory experiments for which he became famous. Since those early days, telepathy, out-of-the-body experiences (OOBES), PK, dreams and metal bending have been studied in laboratories all over the world. And still the scientific establishment tends to sneer and withhold its financial support.

Before laying the blame squarely at the door of sceptical scientists, it is worthwhile considering a point raised by Dr Charles Tart of the University of California during the fifth International Conference of the SPR in Bristol in 1981. He proposed the theory that scepticism about the existence of psi was

Trial and error

'I felt as if the whole framework with which I viewed the world had suddenly been destroyed. I seemed very naked and vulnerable, surrounded by a hostile, incomprehensible universe.' So said John Taylor, well-respected professor of mathematics at London's King's College, in 1973 after witnessing Uri Geller bending metal through mind power alone.

With the characteristic fervour of a convert, Taylor threw himself into a scientific investigation into the paranormal, especially metal bending. But instead of congratulating him on his open-mindedness his colleagues ridiculed and openly ostracised him. So, ironically, it was the scientific establishment, not paranormal phenomena, that ultimately made Taylor's world 'hostile'. He began an attempt to explain metal bending as a function of electromagnetics. When this failed he denounced the entire paranormal spectrum as nonsense or the product of fraud.

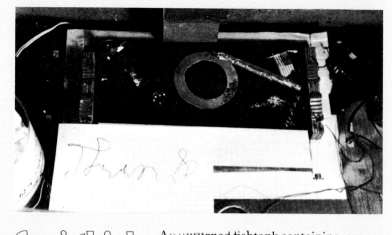

Cox's think tank

An upturned fishtank containing, among other things, separate leather rings, a pen and blank paper – this is the world's most exciting new parapsychological tool, the 'Cox's mini-lab'.

Pioneered in the 1960s by William E. Cox of the Society for Research on Rapport and Telekenesis (SORRAT) at Rolla, Missouri, USA, this simple kit has produced astonishing evidence of PK. 'Encouraged' by the presence of one or more sensitives the leather rings have linked and unlinked, while teleporting from inside to outside the mini-lab, and the pen has written by itself on the paper provided (above). The activities in the lab triggered a movie camera to provide a permanent record.

By 1981 parapsychologists in other parts of the world were building their own mini-labs amid growing anticipation from researchers in the field.

Above left: it has been suggested that it would further the cause of parapsychology as an academic subject if a 'permanent paranormal object' – such as rings linked by PK – could be found and put on display in a museum. Is this such an object? The shapes, cut out of plywood, are firmly linked, but the question is how this came about. Were they ingeniously made that way or were they linked paranormally?

not only entrenched in our rationalist world but is, to a certain extent, necessary for society to function at all. If we 'gave in' to what he believes to be a natural ability – telepathy – and we could all read each other's minds, politics, commerce and personal relationships would fall apart. Scepticism about, and indeed actual resistance to, psi has kept civilisation together.

There is also evidence to show that believers in psi (known in parapsychological jargon as 'sheep') perform random ESP tests more successfully than unbelievers ('goats'). This has been proved time and again in laboratory tests; the 'hits' are significantly higher for sheep than for goats. So we come to a momentous conclusion: an openness to psi tends to encourage phenomena, whereas scepticism quells them. A sceptic will, in fact, appear to prove his prejudice, but then so will a believer. Dr Tart further pointed out to an august assembly of professional and amateur parapsychologists that workers in their own field were not immune to scepticism. Researchers into psi were just as likely as anyone else in our civilisation to exhibit the social fear of strange phenomena. This is

frequently shown, he claimed, by their results; such as scoring 'marginally above chance' in ESP card guessing, enough to justify further study perhaps but not enough to shake the world – or themselves. But those researchers who have successfully faced their ingrained fear of psi and 'trained it out' of themselves have had the most remarkable results. However, one has to be a very thick-skinned and single-minded researcher to be open-minded enough to encourage spectacular psi results.

It is safer and, many would say, more scientific to try to investigate the paranormal purely in terms of the known laws of physics. This may be a rather arrogant approach, assuming as it does that our knowledge of such laws is complete.

But science is based on cautious evaluation, and caution in a field notorious for past frauds and hoaxes is no bad thing. Besides, scientific 'goats' demand watertight evidence for the alleged phenomena, and it is true that there is no theoretical explanation for psychic phenomena that can be tested and developed. Researchers have had notions and ideas about the underlying force responsible for these phenomena, but nothing as substantial as a set of laws has been established. Rhine speculated that there is probably an unknown force or energy – psi – at work. What its characteristics are, how it behaves, and how it affects the material world, he could not say. It still remains to be discovered.

A source of embarrassment

In addition the scientific establishment demands replication. In any other science if a successful experiment cannot be repeated by other scientists using the same methodology in other laboratories then the results are almost certainly invalid. Apart from anything else, replication rules out the possibility that the results were produced by fraud, collusion between experimenter and subject or any other experimental shortcoming. And here parapsychology faces its greatest obstacle and richest source of embarrassment.

For, as reports of telepathy, precognition, clairvoyance and other psychic phenomena show, paranormal events are mainly spontaneous. There is a wayward elusiveness about them. You may, as it were, take your psychic horse to water, but you cannot necessarily make him drink. Metal benders may produce astonishing effects in their own homes, but put them in a laboratory and you may wait until doomsday for a spoon as much as to twitch.

But parapsychology and controllable experiments are not incompatible. John Hasted, professor of physics at Birkbeck College, London, has run a continuing series of experiments on metal bending over several years. Since his investigation of Uri Geller's abilities in the early 1970s he has studied the strange powers of several other gifted youngsters. Despite the scorn of his colleagues he persevered and has devised experiments that he believes have provided important data. Nevertheless, he is fully aware that the phenomena cannot always be produced – or, more significantly, *reproduced* – to order, and his work has involved many hours of patient waiting. His experience as a psychical researcher has taught him to take a more flexible approach; he will often go to the subject's home and encourage the phenomena there rather than plunge the youngster into a clinical atmosphere at the laboratory.

A further problem is the resistance to positive results. When American parapsychologists Harold Puthoff and Russell Targ published the results of their successful 'remote viewing' experiment – to see whether subjects could 'see' and describe by means of ESP a site visited by a target team – they met with a storm of protest from both within and without the parapsychological fraternity. They were accused of bad methodology and poor analysis of data. They refuted the criticisms in a detailed reply. Subsequently similar experiments have been run elsewhere – with positive results.

Guessing which light

Another experiment that has yielded promising results is based on the use of a random number generator. This machine, first developed for the purpose by Helmut Schmidt of the University of Freiburg in West Germany, turns coloured lights on and off in a random sequence while the subject attempts to predict – or even influence – which light will come next. Schmidt has claimed significant results over 10 years of experiments with the machine and one or two other laboratories have also succeeded in producing positive results.

But predicting the colour of the next light or the shape on the next Zener card inevitably means long and often intensely boring hours, days and even weeks in a laboratory. And whereas the technicians involved may be used to such an uninspiring environment, the subjects frequently find their surroundings bleak, intimidating and negative. All this tends to inhibit the very phenomena they seek to bring forth.

One of the few experimental processes that actively encourages the subject to perform in a pleasurable atmosphere uses the 'Ganzfeld' technique. This involves three participants: an agent, who attempts to transmit an image by telepathic means; a subject (or receiver) in the Ganzfeld state – totally relaxed under a soft, diffused light, sensory deprivation and muted white noise; and an experimenter, who records the subject's spoken impressions (or 'mentation') during the transmission period.

One of the leading exponents of experiments based on the Ganzfeld technique is Dr Carl Sargent of Cambridge University,

Above: Helmut Schmidt of the University of Freiburg, West Germany, demonstrates the random number generator he developed for use in ESP tests. Subjects attempt to guess or even influence a sequence of flashing lights; over several years a number of remarkable 'hits' have been scored

Below: Stephen North, the young English boy who has proved to be one of Professor John Hasted's 'star' metal benders

England, who is concerned that the subjects enjoy the experience, that it should be *fun*. He is an exuberant advocate of the positive approach to parapsychology and so far his results have been outstanding. For example, one target image was William Blake's painting *The ancient of days* (showing God kneeling and holding a huge pair of compasses). The sender transmitted the thought 'dividers hurtling through space' and wrote it down on a piece of paper, which was then sealed in an envelope. The subject said he got the impression of 'dividers hurtling through space'. This type of success appears to be most common among experimenters who *encourage* positive results.

Naturally a run of such startlingly successful experiments lays itself open to accusations of bad methodology and even downright collusion between subject and experimenter. While insisting that he takes the most stringent precautions against fraud, Dr Sargent declares that the most important aspect of the experiment is the phenomena, not 'what the neighbours think'.

There will always be critics, including those who doubt the evidence of their own eyes, and the new mood among researchers is to aim first to get the phenomena. Doubts about replication of results, fraud-proof test conditions and assessment of significance over chance must all come afterwards.

The phenomena must come first; without them there is nothing to investigate and the subject becomes unreal. If studying real phenomena attracts academic scorn, then working on secondhand data – hearsay – would make parapsychology a mockery.

And judging by the evidence, the future of psychical research, or more properly, parapsychology, may hang more on the attitude of the researchers themselves than on that of their academic standing.

Few paranormal effects are as controversial as metal bending. But while sceptics dismiss it as fraud or delusion, examples of this bizarre power continue to be recorded. GUY LYON PLAYFAIR tells the story

ACCOUNTS OF INEXPLICABLE contortions of metal objects date back at least to the 18th century, when pins were found twisted into 'a vast variety of fantastic figures' during a poltergeist case, while in 1879 victims of an American case reported that spoons 'suddenly twisted out of shape' in their hands. But it was not until 1972, with the arrival of Uri Geller on the international scene, that paranormal or psychokinetic metal bending (PKMB) – the influencing of metal apparently by mind power alone – became a field of study in its own right.

Over the next four years Geller took part in supervised experiments in 17 different laboratories. Dr George Owen of the New Horizons Research Foundation in Toronto pronounced his abilities as 'paranormal and totally genuine', while Eldon Byrd of the US Navy research centre in Maryland stated that Geller had bent metal under observation 'in a way that cannot be duplicated'. Five professional magicians testified that, despite allegations to the contrary by their colleague James Randi, whatever Geller was doing, it was not conventional stage magic.

After Geller's first television appearance in Britain in 1973, an epidemic of PKMB broke out in homes over the whole country,

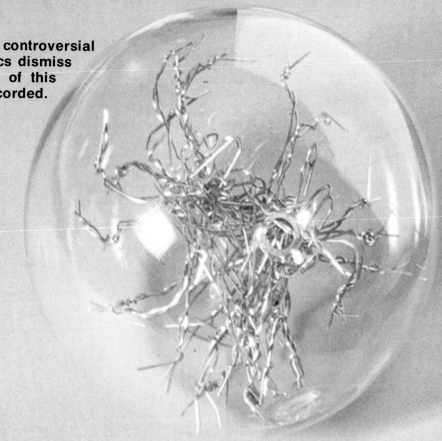

Paperclips dropped into this glass ball were paranormally 'scrunched' into a fantastic shape by one of Professor Hasted's metal bending subjects

Mind over metal

especially affecting young children and teenagers. For some it was a new game soon forgotten (as annoyed parents ran out of usable cutlery), while other children were encouraged to work at it. In 1974, 18-year-old Matthew Manning, then coming to the end of his period as a poltergeist victim, put on a spectacular display of PKMB in front of 21 scientists, including Nobel Laureate Professor Brian Josephson, and enabled psychiatrist Dr Joel Whitton to identify a hitherto unknown brainwave pattern apparently linked to paranormal activity.

But the first scientist to commit himself to a thorough and long-term enquiry into PKMB was Professor J. B. Hasted, head of the physics department of Birkbeck College, London, who carried out a series of tests with several young subjects, both in his laboratory and in the children's homes. Although in the course of his investigations he introduced more rigidly conventional methodology, he soon realised that successful PKMB depends on many other, more subtle factors: for example, the psychological atmosphere in the laboratory was crucial, the state of mind of both subject and experimenter being a decisive factor. Metal benders, he discovered, had to be treated as *colleagues* rather than as guinea-pigs. In an article he co-authored in *Nature* (10 April 1975), he declared that 'psychokinetic phenomena cannot in general be produced unless all who participate are in a relaxed state.' PKMB was, he assumed, a function of the unconscious mind, and too much conscious effort would upset the process, as would an atmosphere of tension, scepticism or hostility. The PKMB

researcher should, he argued, adopt the attitude of a physiotherapist encouraging a patient to regain the use of a damaged limb, rather than telling him it could not be done.

The possibility of trickery had to be eliminated, and to this end Hasted devised experiments in which the metal object was attached to a strain gauge and a chart recorder. And (most important) the subject was not allowed to touch the metal at all. Three of his young colleagues were soon able to produce stress signals on the chart paper under these conditions, signals quite unlike those produced when metal is bent by normal physical force.

'Impossible' tasks

Next, Hasted set his subjects a series of 'impossible' tasks, such as the 'scrunching' together of straightened paperclips inside a glass sphere and the bending of alloy strips that snap rather than bend under normal stresses. Again, the young subjects responded to these challenges, producing a number of remarkable scrunches, while one managed to deform four strips of 'unbendable' alloy merely by leaving them, untouched, in his coat pocket for five minutes. By December 1976, Hasted was able to state categorically, in the *Journal* of the Society for Psychical Research (SPR): 'I therefore report my belief that I have been able to validate the metal-bending phenomenon on a number of occasions by visual witnessing, chart-recording, "impossible" tasks and the bending of brittle metals.'

The following year, in the same journal, he described a series of 13 tests held with 17-year-old Nicholas Williams, the highlight of which was the chart recording of simultaneous strain signals from three different keys hanging from wires, and even from two metal objects 10 yards (9 metres) apart on different floors of the building. Eventually, Hasted was able to add some sequences of videotape to his evidence, in which metal objects can be seen bending without being touched. The PKMB phenomenon had, it seemed, been well and truly validated.

It had also been repeated in several other countries, under the supervision of qualified researchers. At the Péchiney Laboratory in France, metallurgists Professor Charles Crussard and Dr Jean Bouvaist published a detailed report on the abilities of Jean Pierre Girard, the most thoroughly studied of all metal benders. They found that he could induce both anomalous hardening and softening in metal in a manner impossible to explain in terms of conventional metallurgy. Girard, who was born in 1942, developed numerous psychic abilities shortly after being struck by lightning as a child.

He made his début as a metal bender in 1975, in response to a radio appeal from Dr William Wolkowski for people with psi abilities to come forward. He successfully distorted a number of metal samples, including

Above: a metal bar fitted with strain gauges and then bent paranormally in Professor Hasted's London laboratory. A chart recorder was also attached to the metal and, to eliminate the possibility of trickery, the subjects were not allowed to touch the metal. It still bent, showing stress signals unlike those produced when attempts were made to bend the bar manually

Right: Professor John Hasted checks strain gauge equipment in the laboratory

Previous page: seven-year-old Mark Shelley bent cutlery after seeing 'that man' – Uri Geller – on television in October 1973. He went on to prove his new skill on more household cutlery before tiring of metal bending. He said: 'It seems a waste of time going around the world like this. I'd rather play football for Ipswich'

a steel spring, sealed inside glass tubes under Wolkowski's supervision. In one of his most dramatic demonstrations of PKMB, he bent a 3-inch (8-centimetre) screw inside a plastic tube held by Swedish physicist Dr Georg Wikman in about 15 seconds, without touching either the screw or the tube.

In West Germany, Professor Hans Bender of the University of Freiburg studied Girard with the co-operation of William Cox – well-known parapsychologist and magician – and a cameraman, and became one of the first to record PKMB on film. Girard produced more than 10 distinct bends under close scrutiny, but in fairly informal conditions. (Two French magicians, Ranky and André Sanlaville, have testified that his effects are not produced by conventional sleight of hand.) By 1977, Girard had demonstrated his abilities in front of at least 16 scientists.

Professor Bender also filmed an adult Swiss, Silvio Meyer, as he bent several spoons by PK alone, breaking some of them in the process, and also bending several heavy forks *upwards* while holding each lightly with only one hand. Meanwhile, in Japan, several children developed PKMB talents after Geller's visit to Tokyo in 1973, and two of them – Masuaki Kiyota and Jun Sekiguchi – were studied at length by several scientists, notably Professor Shigemi Sasaki of the Department of Electro-Communications, Tokyo University, and Dr Matsumi Suzuki of the Aeronautical Instruments Research Institute.

As the evidence from laboratories all over

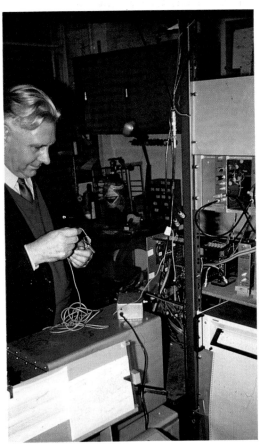

the world mounted up, support came from theoretical physicists who found that not only was 'action at a distance' permitted according to the laws of quantum physics, but it could actually be predicted. At a conference on 'Frontiers of Physics' held in Iceland in 1977 it became clear, amid talk of 'collapsing wave functions', 'intrinsic time symmetry' and 'additivity of partial amplitudes', that the human mind had been willingly accepted as a potential influence on physical processes. PKMB had become almost respectable.

The phenomenon has also come to the attention of psychiatrists, and in a lengthy study of young metal benders and their families, Dr Robert Cantor found that most youngsters also showed other paranormal abilities, from telepathy and clairvoyance to healing. Some had also seen tiny lights moving around them, and heard high-pitched whistles. Others reported experiencing headaches while concentrating on bending metal (as did some of their investigators), plus tingling sensations in the arms and face. Cantor also found that PKMB seemed to have no harmful effects, and actually served to increase the children's self-confidence. Most encouraging of all was the fact that all children he questioned insisted that their powers must be used for good. If misused, they felt, they would lose them. The experience of one of them serves as an answer to the often-asked question: 'Who needs bent spoons anyway?'

Belinda H. was only six when she responded to Uri Geller's invitation to bend metal during the transmission of BBC-TV's *Blue Peter* programme. She deformed a spoon through 40° in less than a minute, and

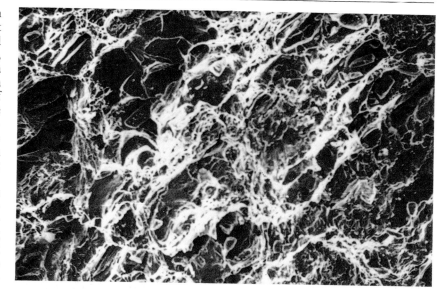

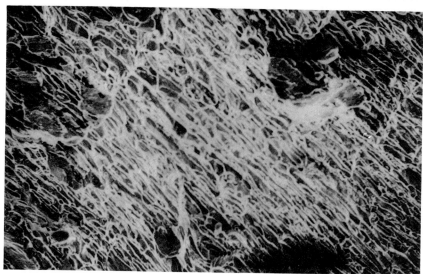

Scanning electron microscope photographs – magnified 750 times – of (top) a section of a Volkswagen key that broke when Geller tried to bend it and (above) of a similar key broken by mechanical means. The paranormally broken key shows a uniform structure, the other key a random pattern

Left: George Porter with some of the objects he bent by PK while listening to Uri Geller on the *Jimmy Young Show* on BBC radio in 1974

later bent an 'unbendable' crystal in the presence of Professor Hasted. (She looked set to win the *Daily Express* £5,000 metal-bending contest until this was mysteriously cancelled.) However, Belinda was more interested in healing. When she was only three years old she had spontaneously tried to cure her ailing grandmother, and on three other occasions she satisfied both her parents that she had been able to relieve severe pain by placing her hands on the affected parts of their bodies.

PKMB has repeatedly been demonstrated to be a fact, and scientists have begun to respond to the challenge it offers. A solution to the age-old mystery of how our minds interact with matter is much nearer than it was when Uri Geller came to public attention in 1972. Jean Pierre Girard feels that PKMB is an evolutionary mechanism necessary for Man's survival that science cannot afford to overlook. From the apparently useless ability to bend spoons there may develop enormously far-reaching effects on the world.

'This power,' says Belinda H.'s mother, 'must have been put there for a reason.'

Testing the healer's gift

Is healing simply a matter of faith, or does the healer really possess a power that can cure diseased tissue? DAVID HARVEY looks at the startling results of some major experiments into this paranormal ability

IF THE LAYING ON of hands and related 'healing' techniques help people to recover from illness, as so many claim, then the process involved should be of major significance. True, the medical profession would have to rethink its attitude towards healing completely, but if we could discover something about the nature of 'faith healing', then the potential benefits would far outweigh the hostility it is likely to incur from the medical establishment. Even if research into the subject revealed only that the healing process were achieved in some relatively mundane way then it would still be of enormous use; for example, in helping established therapists to improve their techniques and encouraging others to learn how to heal.

Unfortunately those involved in the mainstream of science – and medicine in particular – still regard even the most attested healers with suspicion and open hostility. So, as with most parapsychological research, it is only the rare, brave individual bold enough to step outside the confines of orthodox science who dare investigate the subject.

One of the pioneers in this field was a young biochemist, Dr Bernard Grad of McGill University, Montreal, Canada, who, in the late 1950s, decided that the claims

Above: the late Harry Edwards, Britain's foremost spiritual healer of the day, treats a crippled child, watched by a crowd of 6000 people at London's Royal Albert Hall in September 1954. It could be said that by removing the outward symbol of the child's illness – the ugly and constraining leg irons – he is in some way 'shocking' the child into health, in the same way as Christ's 'take up thy bed and walk' healed a paralytic. But are healers more than just clever psychotherapists: do they emit some as yet unnamed force that acts on the body as well as the mind?

made for the efficacy of the laying on of hands were too important to be ignored. He believed that it was a phenomenon that demanded to be investigated.

To Grad, the fact that no one had run experiments on it before was almost as great a mystery as the healing process itself. As he observed, there was no difficulty in applying suitable biomedical procedures to the process of healing. The explanation for the widespread apathy had to lie elsewhere. Perhaps the very simplicity and apparently unsophisticated nature of the healing process represented an affront to a scientific age dedicated to ingenious, technical solutions to medical problems.

However, Grad was not deterred from delving deeper into the subject. Nor was he alarmed, as many suggested he might be, by the problem of sorting out the genuine from

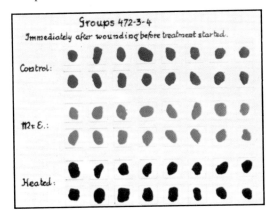

the bogus healers. He argued that if the alleged healer can really heal, this should be obvious from the results obtained under carefully controlled conditions.

Aware of the exciting possibilities ahead, he stated: 'From such studies, it might be possible to develop tests which would distinguish persons with the gift from those without it; and more importantly, it might provide information basic to some aspects of the healing art, namely psychotherapy and the so-called placebo effect.'

Indeed, the discovery of the placebo effect in drug trials had already raised some extremely difficult questions for medical scientists: human beings were not the predictable biochemical machines they had assumed.

Great expectations

When tests are conducted to evaluate the effect of new drugs, a control group is always included. The surprise result on a number of occasions has been that some members of the control group, dosed with plain sugar pills (placebos), have mimicked the physiological response of those who took the actual drugs, a phenomenon known as the placebo effect. Expectation, instilled by taking part in the trials, seems to have been the crucial factor since none of the 'guinea pigs' (and none of the staff who handed out the drugs) knew whether they were receiving sugar pills or the real thing. This type of experiment is known as 'double blind'. So under controlled conditions it has been shown that the mind, primed by suggestion, can influence the body's behaviour to a remarkable degree.

In the early years of the 20th century, the notion that such an interaction could occur was regarded as mere speculation, although many had maintained that the mind-over-body effect was real enough. But interesting though placebo-effect experiments are, Grad considered they did not go far enough. Would his research show that healing depends for its effectiveness on the mysterious power of suggestion? Or would it reveal yet a further layer of complexity in this subtle and imperfectly understood process?

Impressed with the anecdotal evidence for the effectiveness of the laying on of hands, Grad decided to see whether he could devise experiments that would show that this form

Right: Dr Bernard Grad, whose pioneering experiments into the nature of spiritual healing have also provided insights into other aspects of Man's potential. For example, having 'green fingers' may not be a matter of luck, but part of a barely understood gift of regeneration

Below, far left: day one of an experiment to test Oskar Estebany's healing through the 'laying on of hands'. Forty-eight mice were 'wounded' by having a piece of skin removed. Here the wounds can be seen to be fairly uniform in size and degree. Some of the mice were then handled by Estebany twice a day for 20 days. The rest were either left untreated – but put in containers heated to simulate the warmth of human hands – or they were handled by other members of the staff in a manner similar to that of Estebany

Left: day 14 and the wounds of the mice treated by Estebany have healed significantly faster than any of the others

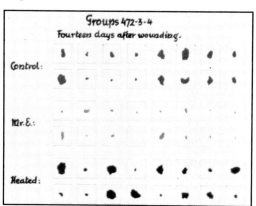

Groups 472-3-4
Fourteen days after wounding.

Control:

Mr. E.:

Heated:

of treatment involved another force or some, as yet undetected, interaction between the healer and patient. The problem was to find a way of successfully isolating one factor from the others. Just as the placebo effect had upset the results of drug trials, so suggestion might interfere with an attempt to find out what is happening when a healer is at work.

Grad quickly concluded that the use of human beings in any experiment would make the task next to impossible: there would always be doubt as to which factors – suggestion or 'faith' – were responsible for any change or improvement. So he chose to use animals and plants for his project. As far as anyone is aware, neither are susceptible to the power of suggestion nor do they have expectations about the purpose of any experiment. From this point of view, Grad felt he would be on safe ground.

The healer he chose to act as the agent for the research was Colonel Oskar Estebany. A retired Hungarian army colonel, he had discovered his healing ability when working with cavalry horses, and then developed his talents with human patients. In later years, healing became his main activity. He asked nothing for his services and made no extravagant claims about what he could achieve. In 1957 he left Hungary and went to live in Canada, and by 1960 he had a paid job in Grad's laboratory.

In the first experiment, 48 mice had a small piece of skin of similar size removed from their backs under anaesthesia. They were then weighed and the dimensions of the wounds measured and recorded. (For two weeks prior to the experiment the mice had been 'gentled' by handling since it had been found that nervous animals made unreliable subjects for research work.) At this stage in the proceedings no one knew which mice were to serve as controls and which were to receive treatment.

After the operation, the mice were divided into three groups, which were placed in separate wire cages. Estebany treated the first group by standing the cage on his left hand and resting his right hand on the top. There was no physical contact with the mice.

The second group was cared for in an identical way in terms of feeding and other routines, but left alone – this was the control group. The third group also received identical care but, instead of being treated by Estebany, the mice were warmed to a temperature comparable to that generated by the healer's hands, to see whether heat alone would accelerate wound healing.

The skin wounds were measured regularly over a period of 20 days so that their recovery rate could be analysed and compared. The mice that had been warmed showed no significant difference in their speed of healing from the control group. The mice treated by Estebany recovered at a much faster rate than chance expectancy.

Could Oskar Estebany's healing power make plants grow faster? Dr Grad set up a simple experiment to test this possibility: barley seeds were planted in two groups of pots, labelled X and Y. Both groups were watered with a weak saline solution, but group X was watered with a solution that Estebany had held, in a flask, for 30 minutes. Group Y was watered normally by a member of staff. By day 10 (below left) group X was already significantly taller and stronger than the control group, and by day 14 (below right) the difference was even more marked

a special healing ability. Once more, those treated by Estebany showed the most rapid rate of recovery.

From these results, Grad felt that he was on the verge of a significant discovery – but where was it leading? To clarify this, his next goal was to learn more about the underlying mechanism involved. If there were some healing force at work, as the animal experiments seemed to prove, there was no reason to suppose that it should be effective only on the animal kingdom. To discover whether any measurable effects could be registered using plants as the healing target, Grad devised an experiment to see if Estebany could influence the germination and rate of growth of barley seeds. And, if successful, the experiment would presumably throw further light on the mechanism involved.

To begin with, Grad watered the seeds with a weak saline solution. The pots, already numbered, containing the seeds were dried out, stood in rows and watered.

The only variable factor in the treatment of the seeds was that some pots were watered with a saline solution that had been held by Estebany. That was the only part he played

The scars of the mice treated by the healer had shrunk almost uniformly to pencil-point size. Those of the mice in the other groups showed varying stages of healing; some scars were as small as those in Estebany's group but about half were markedly larger.

But however promising the results from this one experiment might look, they cannot be regarded as a breakthrough. As in any scientific experiment, replication of results by other laboratories is an important check on the soundness of the procedures and therefore on the validity of the results.

A similar experiment to Grad's was staged at the University of Manitoba, also in Canada. This time it involved a total of 300 mice. Double-blind conditions were incorporated into the project to avoid any possibility of unconscious manipulation by the experimenters. As a further check, one group of mice was 'treated' – copying Estebany's procedure – by people who made no claim to

in the experiment. There was no direct contact between the healer and the seeds or pots. More of those that had been watered with the 'treated' saline solution germinated faster, grew quicker and healthier than the control group.

Grad wondered if the results could be attributable to bacterial growth present in the water and encouraged by the warmth of the healer's hands, but this seemed impossible because only sterile, saline solutions had been used. Grad concluded that there probably was an independent, beneficial force involved, something that could penetrate a barrier of glass and affect the properties of the solution inside.

There were other variables to consider. He had isolated a specific effect for which the healer appeared to be responsible, although Grad was unable to demonstrate exactly what was happening. Even so, there was another aspect of the process that seemed to be worth exploring: the psychological condition of the healer under which this 'force' or 'energy' could be best transmitted.

Taking note that Estebany and other healers maintained that a calm, tranquil frame of mind was a prerequisite for healing to take place, Grad selected three people with obviously different psychological states to treat the saline solution before running the barley seed test. He hypothesised that if the healer had a positive effect on the solution, and thence the seeds, there should be a different result according to the state of mind of the individual.

Of the three people he chose, J. B. was psychiatrically normal, with a reputation for being a 'green-fingered' gardener. The other two, R. H. and H. R., were both disturbed and under psychiatric care. What Grad was looking for was evidence of a differential germination and growth rate: a higher yield from the positive and confident individual compared with the other two participants in the experiment. Each held a sealed flask of sterile saline solution for half an hour and then the experiment proceeded as before; the control set of flasks was not touched by any one. The man with green fingers achieved a significantly higher germination and growth rate than the others.

A disturbing effect

Pondering on the results of the seed experiment, Grad returned to his earlier supposition that people who were disturbed would have a negative effect on the seeds. He believed that there were still further lessons to be teased from the exercise. Was there any explanation why R. H.'s seeds grew relatively more vigorously than those in the untreated control group, and those of H. R. less so?

On questioning them on their attitude and state of mind at the time when they were treating the water, Grad learned that R. H., a

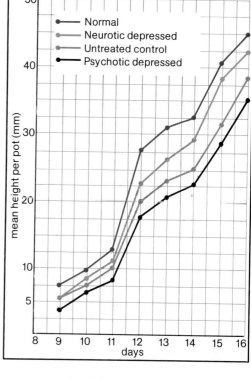

The significant difference in the growth rate of seedlings treated by Oskar Estebany and those treated similarly by ordinary laboratory staff over a number of days can be seen in the chart (below). But can mentally disturbed people have a dramatically different effect on growing plants? Dr Grad set up a test involving one clinically neurotic patient, one psychotic patient and, as a control, a normal person. Each had to hold, water and care for the same number of pots containing seedlings. The results of these tests (right) seem conclusive. In some way (as yet unknown) the positive mood of a normal person can encourage the growth of organic matter and, more significantly, certain people – 'healers' – can somehow accelerate its healthy growth

woman, had suddenly perked up and shown an active interest when informed of the purpose of the experiment, and had cradled the flask in her lap. In contrast, H. R.'s mood remained agitated and depressed. This, for Grad, proved the point that it was not the individual's usual, everyday disposition, but that which prevails at the *time* of the experiment that seemed to be the factor.

While Grad had not finally resolved the question of what was responsible for changes that resulted from the laying on of hands, he believed he could advance some conclusions: first, from the mice and barley experiments, he felt that there was evidence that the laying on of hands could induce cell growth and that the way in which this occurred suggested the action of some kind of energy that was not merely heat. Second, he concluded from the differing results achieved by the psychiatrically normal and the disturbed subjects that there was a damming or releasing control associated with the individual's state of mind at the time of the experiment.

Grad speculated further. He wondered whether these experiments underlined the importance of rapport between therapist and patient which, when strong and positive, involved the transfer or generation of some energy that aided the healing process.

Like so much pioneering research, Grad's work raised many questions, all of central importance to medicine and Man. His experiments also inspired other scientists to pick up the trail themselves. Several have reported findings that corroborate those claims made by Grad for some independent healing energy, and the search goes on. Whether or not that energy will be tracked down, we shall have to wait and see.

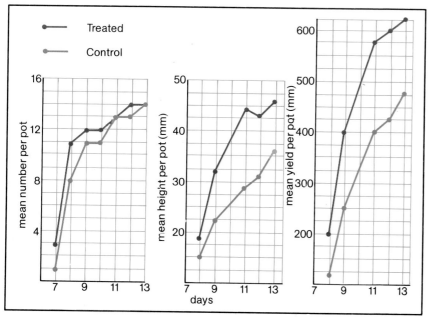

Can the mind somehow travel many miles, tour a target location and report back with an accurate description? This chapter discusses the controversial claims made for the phenomenon of remote viewing

WHEN RUSSELL TARG and Harold Puthoff published *Mind-reach* in 1977 they were not modest about its claims: they had, they asserted, made the final breakthrough and established scientifically that the phenomenon known as remote viewing was fact, and they considered it to be 'probably a latent and widely distributed perceptual ability.'

Remote viewing – a kind of ESP – was not a new subject for discussion and experiment. Papers covering aspects of the phenomenon had appeared in the early 1970s in the British science journal *Nature* and in other highly respected publications. Although controversial, it was believed to be a subject to be taken seriously, and Targ and Puthoff's work in this field especially so, for they were both established physicists on the academic staff of California's Stanford Research Institute (SRI).

Their standing as reputable scientists and the confident way they presented their case made it impossible to ignore their claims. Their research was subjected to intense

Left: ESP experimenter Serena Roney-Dougal's experiments involve information sent in ways not perceptible by the ordinary senses of the subject. Here, the sender listens to a tape and tries to communicate the information on it by telepathy

Russell Targ (left) and Harold Puthoff (right), respected physicists of California's Stanford Research Institute. But their pioneering work into remote viewing was savagely attacked by scientists and psychical researchers alike

scrutiny – and the reaction they received was little short of savage.

Targ and Puthoff were accused of everything from deliberately misreading the results and prompting the subjects to unscientific methodology. Even so, they invited other scientists to try to reproduce their results; indeed, since 1977 many others have tried, and with very little success. To many psychical researchers it seemed that remote viewing, like so many other similar 'breakthroughs', was a kind of mirage. Was it possible that the researchers trying to reproduce the results of Targ and Puthoff's work had missed some element in the experiments? Or was it that the two physicists had, in their enthusiasm, pushed their conclusions too far?

Targ and Puthoff began their experiments with a series of remarkable successes, using as subjects New York artist and psychic Ingo Swann and retired police commissioner Pat Price. Both showed remarkable aptitude for remote viewing; in some cases they even named the target location instead of merely describing it. Sometimes they were given only map co-ordinates and asked to describe in detail what they 'saw'.

These and other successes inspired Targ and Puthoff to mount more tightly controlled experiments to validate beyond doubt the

View from afar

claimed his 'description is accurate in almost every detail'.

Indeed, Price's 'viewing' contained much that was specifically relevant to the arts and crafts plaza. He said, for example, 'I'm looking at something that looks like an arbor. . . . Seems to be cool, shaded. Doesn't seem to me that they're [i.e. the target team] out in the direct sunlight. . . . there's lots of trees, in an arbor area.'

Startlingly accurate though much of this was, many of Price's transcripts also included much that was incorrect. The researchers began to see a pattern in his remote viewing, noting 'the occurrence of essentially correct descriptions of basic elements and patterns coupled with incomplete or erroneous analysis of function was to be a continuing thread throughout the remote viewing work.' In other words, he was often muddled or wrong.

phenomenon of remote viewing.

Altogether there were nine experiments using Pat Price, which were duly written up and published in *Nature* in October 1974. In these a high proportion of the transcript description is very specific; some might have thought suspiciously so. Perhaps it was for this very reason that this series provoked the most hostile reaction.

Price had been set nine target locations in the Stanford area; these were noted down, and each was sealed in an envelope before being locked away in a safe. Pat Price and an experimenter – usually Russell Targ – stationed themselves in a room about 30 minutes before remote viewing was due to begin. Meanwhile Harold Puthoff, together with at least one other member of the target team, selected an envelope at random from the safe, opened it, and set off for the specified location. Neither Price nor Targ had any communication with the rest of the team from the very beginning of the test.

A perfect description

The first site was a well-known landmark on the Stanford campus, the Hoover Tower. Not only did Price immediately describe a tower-like structure, but actually specified it as the 'Hoover Tower'.

This seemed almost too good to be true. The protocol of the experiments was then tightened to prevent any security leaks. The divisional director, whose function it was to open the target envelope, now drove the team to the site *before* revealing its identity to them. The first time they did this the target was Redwood City Marina. Price's first taped words were: 'What I'm looking at is a little boat jetty or . . . dock along the bay.'

Another bull's eye description was given for the seventh target on the list: an arts and crafts plaza with shops, flowers, ceramic ornaments, fountains, paths and vine-hung arbors. In the report Price's unedited transcript is quoted verbatim. Targ and Puthoff

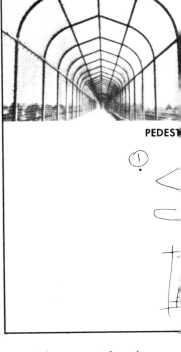

Top: a student tests his ESP ability using a machine devised by Targ and Puthoff. The subject has to indicate which image is going to flash on a screen seconds before it appears. This apparatus is also used in psi testing by Professor Hans Bender and Elmar Gruber of the Freiburg Institute in West Germany

He also, they noted, drew target locations or objects as mirror images, which proved – to them – that the right hemisphere of the brain was somehow involved in the process, for the right side of the brain is believed to control holistic, pattern-making and intuitive thinking.

Impressive as Price's results were to those who worked with him closely, the real test came when the transcripts and drawings were compared with the target areas by an independent judge who visited the nine sites and then rated the descriptions on a scale of one to nine, best to worst match. He had been presented with Price's unlabelled narratives in a random order, so he had no hint as to which site Price had been referring – except from the scripts themselves. Having carried out this evaluation, the judge awarded him

Right: the late Dr Kit Pedler with biologist Dr Beverley Rubik at the target selected for a remote viewing test, Indian Rock, Berkeley, California, in 1980. Although the subject – many miles away – noted a few correspondences with the target, most of her report described Codornices Park, which she later verified by visiting it. Dr Pedler did not consider this a complete 'miss' but was convinced that she had, in some way, 'seen' the park through the displacement effect that is so often noted by researchers. This in itself raises further perplexing questions

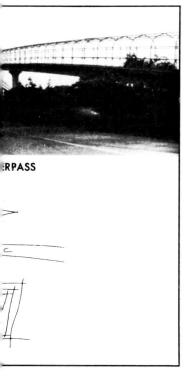

Above: Hella Hammid's drawing of the target that she described as 'some kind of diagonal trough up in the air'. Compare it with the target, a pedestrian overpass; the perspective is particularly accurate

Above left: a sketch of a target as 'seen' by one of the SRI subjects, and a photograph of the actual location – San Andres airport in Colombia, South America. It is a remarkable 'hit'

seven direct hits out of nine, a strikingly significant result, the odds against this happening by chance being at least 35,000:1.

A further back-up was provided when a separate group of SRI scientists, so far unassociated with the Targ/Puthoff programme, were asked to match the scripts against the targets. The same procedure followed as before: unlabelled, randomly ordered transcripts were distributed to the team of five, who then visited the sites independently.

Chance alone would have provided five correct matches overall, but in this test, the correct correlation was much higher: individually the investigation team scored them seven, six, five, three and three.

The fascinating aspect about Price's involvement was that he, although obviously a successful 'viewer', did not claim to possess any special gift for it, merely saying that he was willing to give the experiments a try. If it were true that he had no special 'talent' and yet was so strikingly successful, the researchers wondered if anyone could do it.

They found a suitable guinea-pig for the next stage in the series in Hella Hammid, a professional photographer. Another nine-experiment series was mounted, along similar lines to that using Price. The only difference was that Hammid's remote viewing time was cut from 30 to 15 minutes.

Drawing conclusions

Hammid preferred to make drawings of her mental impressions, rather than describe them verbally as Price had done. Some of these 'doodles' were remarkably accurate.

Again an independent judge was brought in to repeat the matching process and the results were just as impressive: five direct hits and four second ranks. The odds against this were given as 500,000:1.

Following up this success, Targ and Puthoff ran a further four series of tests involving seven other subjects. All but one test proved to be statistically significant.

These results should indeed, as *Mindreach* claimed, have proved beyond a shadow of a doubt that remote viewing is *fact*. However, the experiments and their results were not always straightforward nor easy to evaluate. For example, when the late Dr Kit Pedler was making his series *Mind over matter* for British television he visited Stanford and took part in an experiment himself, and certain problems emerged.

Hella Hammid acted as subject while Dr Pedler and Dr Beverley Rubik, a biologist who had joined up with the team for the experiment, drove off to one of the six randomly selected sites in the vicinity. Television viewers saw Pedler and Rubik wandering round a rocky incline, while Hammid – locked in a hotel room – was being filmed speaking and drawing her mental impressions of what they were seeing.

After a specified period Pedler and Rubik

returned to the hotel and compared notes with Hammid. Then Hammid was driven to each of the six sites with the task of identifying the target with only her previously recorded impressions as guides. As it happened, she was convinced she had not 'seen' the target – but instead identified one of the other sites on the list, Codornices Park, as the place she had 'seen'.

Dr Pedler found the very nature of this 'miss' intriguing. Though some may think his reasoning merely desperate rationalisation in an embarrassing situation, he pointed out that there is a well-known, if little understood, factor called the 'displacement effect'. This is an extremely mysterious process, found also in other telepathic experiments, which operates when the subject homes in, not on the target itself, but on one of the others in the target pool. The phenomenon frequently goes unremarked because researchers are concerned solely with totalling up direct hits. To many, including Dr Pedler, this aspect of telepathic experiment was potentially just as exciting as getting direct hits all the time.

But in the case of the Puthoff/Targ experiments more mundane objections were also raised. On only very few occasions was the received image unambiguously clear. There may indeed be a number of correct correspondences, but in most cases there is an abundance of over-generalised description: trees, roads, flowers, hills and so on – easily guessed components of many likely target sites. Sifting out the relevant from the 'padding', agreeing on the significance of each phrase in the transcript is clearly not quite as easy as the experimenters stated.

Yet, despite these quibbles, Targ and Puthoff did seem to present a strikingly positive case for remote viewing. So why did the critics attack them so fiercely?

Not only sceptical scientists but also fellow psychical researchers took issue with Targ and Puthoff over their remote viewing experiments at SRI. But why?

THE RESEARCH BY Russell Targ and Harold Puthoff into remote viewing certainly made an impact. For many people on the fringe of parapsychology, including students and interested laymen, their work had the full weight of authority behind it, for both men were physicists of some standing. If they were prepared to put their reputations at risk by stating so positively that remote viewing *exists*, then who could doubt the validity of their work? However, their fellow scientists, many of them prejudiced against parapsychology in the first place, and some who were merely cautious, were not so ready to hail the results as a breakthrough.

Two of the sceptics were David Marks and Richard Kamman, both psychologists at New Zealand's Otago University. Their students, reading of Puthoff and Targ's conclusions, had begun to bombard them with questions about remote viewing and parapsychology in general. The Stanford Research Institute (SRI) had suddenly become the centre of attention.

Neither Marks nor Kamman had, until that point in the late 1970s, any special interest in ESP and they admitted their relative ignorance about parapsychology. But the pressure from their students was so intense that they realised they would have to learn. They were interested in the SRI experiments particularly because Targ and Puthoff had claimed that almost anyone, psychically gifted or not, could be successful in remote viewing tests. It was also claimed that the results of the experiments were easy to reproduce.

So, between 1976 and 1978, Marks and Kamman ran 35 trials similar to the SRI

Close-up on remote viewing

In an article written in 1927 Sir Oliver Lodge cited as evidence for 'telepathy at a distance' the case of the Misses Miles and Ramsden. They undertook a series of experiments in telepathy, which were similar to those carried out in the 1970s at SRI. Miss Miles photographed Henbury Church in Cheshire (above), while Miss Ramsden, in Scotland, drew her mental impressions of the image being transmitted (left). Miss Ramsden, however, felt dissatisfied, saying 'something is wanting, as it seemed bigger and more imposing'. The general shape is correct but the lack of ivy and the slit windows suggest she had somehow 'picked up' an early version of the church

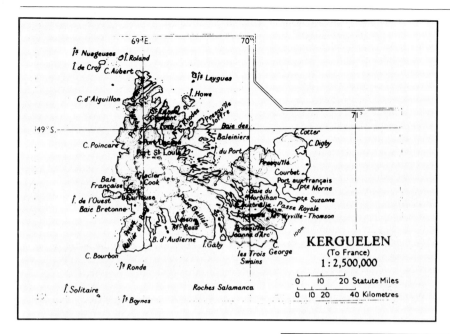

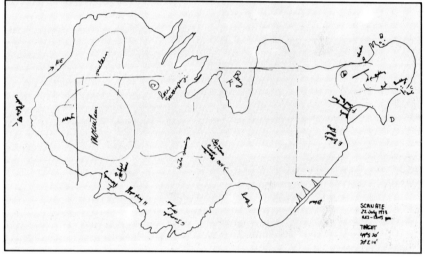

judges can't match my descriptions accurately, there will be something wrong with them.'

Unfortunately this confidence was misplaced – the independent judges, brought in to try to match transcripts with actual target locations, failed to do so in every case they were asked to consider.

Up to this stage everyone at Otago had felt very positive about the outcome of the experiments; so what had gone wrong? Marks and Kamman decided to accompany one subject and the target group on one of their joint trips to the target location after the actual remote viewing had taken place. This was to reveal serious flaws in the nature of the experiment – and by implication the experiments of Puthoff and Targ, whose methodology they had followed so carefully. The New Zealanders labelled the problem *subjective validation*; put simply, this means that if you want an experiment to work it will,

sessions. They used five subjects: a graduate psychologist, a hypnotist, a housewife, an arts student and a medical undergraduate. All of them expressed the belief that they had some psychic ability.

Marks and Kamman followed the SRI routines as faithfully as possible. The target team was given 20 minutes to reach its specified destination, then the subject – back at the laboratory – noted down any feelings or impressions about the unknown target for 15 minutes. The team returned, collected the subject and all then went to the target site to check the subject's transcript against the location. Marks and Kamman were pleased to find encouraging correspondences at the early stages of their project. One of their subjects was so confident that he said, 'If the

Project Scanate (scanning by co-ordinate) was one of the most controversial areas of SRI's remote viewing experiments. A map co-ordinate would be given to the team by telephone and the subject asked to describe the location, which would later be checked. According to Puthoff and Targ, psychic Ingo Swann (left) showed remarkable talent for this. The map co-ordinates for Kerguelen Island in the Indian Ocean (top) were given to Swann who responded with an extremely accurate verbal description of the location. His version of the map (above) is, however, much less convincing, especially considering that Swann is also an artist and is used to thinking in visual terms

because you will tend to select the results you were seeking and reject the rest. Since all the subjects had been strongly motivated to succeed, they had tended to grasp at correspondences – between their impressions and the target – that, according to the judges, simply did not exist. 'The fact is,' concluded Marks and Kamman, 'any target can be matched by any description to some degree.'

For their part, the judges had tried hard to match transcripts against targets and they felt they had come up with the best matches possible. Unfortunately they were not the same details seized upon as 'proof' by the experimental team.

The Otago team then asked the obvious question: if we have had this difficulty, then how did Targ and Puthoff manage to achieve so many direct hits? They began to investigate the SRI findings in closer detail and came up with some provocative discoveries about the way the transcripts had been judged.

For example, they noticed that the SRI transcripts were unedited, including all manner of material in addition to the subject's actual narrative. Only some scripts were dated, and others – significantly – carried references to previous experiments. One of Pat Price's transcripts – the Redwood City Marina test (see page 38) – expressly mentions the previous day's target: 'I've been trying to picture it in my mind and where you went yesterday on your nature walk. . . .'

Marks and Kamman saw this as a potential cue to the judge, who was ostensibly trying to evaluate the material on its descriptive content alone. In effect this apparently throwaway remark could be telling the judge that whatever the target was, it was *not* a nature walk, because that was yesterday's target. With such cues the judge could have worked out the series of targets, consciously or subconsciously, and given higher scores as a result.

What the SRI trials had not included, and what they badly needed according to the

Two SRI 'stars' draw their impressions of the target, a typewriter. Ingo Swann's sketch (on the left) seems strikingly accurate, though he did not actually name the object, noting instead that it 'seems to be in two parts, one sitting on top of the other'. Hella Hammid's sketch (on the right) is not impressive although the grid effect could be seen as a keyboard

Otago team, was an attempt at remote *judging*. Was it possible, they wondered, that the judges could come up with good matches armed only with the transcripts – not visiting the target site at all?

The two psychologists acquired five of the Price scripts that had not been published from a consultant to the SRI project. These appeared to be covered in cues such as references to 'yesterday's two targets', more specifically 'the second of the day', and Targ's encouraging comment on one transcript, 'nothing like having three successes behind you'. Other subtle cues included mention of the time of day of the experiment, useful when more than one experiment is staged in one day. In a rigidly controlled scientific experiment there should have been nothing but the subject's impressions on the transcript, and only references to that particular remote viewing session. Any extraneous matter was not only bad methodology, but suspicious.

Right on cue

With a little intelligent guesswork, and a little reading between the – added – lines, Marks correctly matched all five transcripts to the targets, 'solely on the basis of the cues contained in the transcripts, and no visits to target locations . . . prior to the successful matchings.'

Marks and Kamman argued that the SRI judging could hardly be said to have been blind. Their conclusion, as it was published in *Nature*, says:

> Our investigation of the SRI remote viewing experiment with Pat Price forces the conclusion that the successful identification of target sites by judges is impossible unless multiple extraneous cues which were available in the original unedited transcripts are utilized. Investigators of remote viewing should take more care to ensure that such cues are not available. Furthermore, the listing of targets given to judges should be randomized and not presented in the same sequence as that which occurred in the experiments.

And what about the astonishingly successful SRI remote viewing tests using Ingo Swann and Hella Hammid? On balance, Marks and Kamman seriously doubted whether tighter controls had been involved in those. Their final, damning verdict, published in their book *The psychology of the psychic* (1980), is that 'It appears to us that the remote viewing effect is, at present, nothing more than a massive artifact of poor methodology and wishful thinking.'

They did admit that they had been working with incomplete data and, of course, they had not been present during the SRI tests.

However, Robert Morris, who reviewed *The psychology of the psychic* in the *Journal* of the American Society for Psychical Research (ASPR), investigated the New Zealanders'

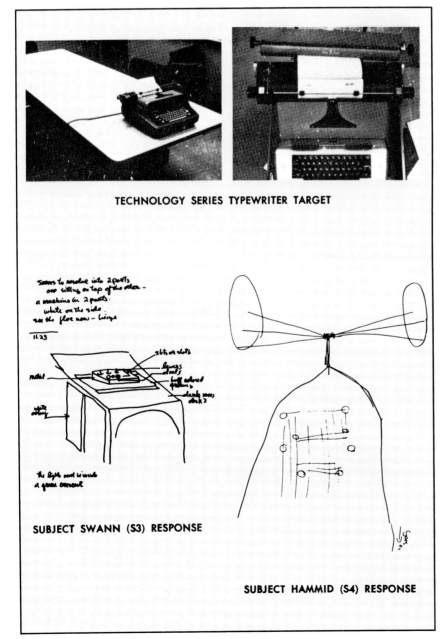

TECHNOLOGY SERIES TYPEWRITER TARGET

SUBJECT SWANN (S3) RESPONSE

SUBJECT HAMMID (S4) RESPONSE

One such case took place during one of Dr Carol Sargent's Ganzfeld sensory deprivation tests at Cambridge, England in June 1981. Peter Brookesmith (Editor of *The Unexplained*) acted as 'sender' and Lynn Picknett (Deputy Editor) as subject. A target picture (left) was chosen from four randomly selected, sealed envelopes, yet the subject received vivid and detailed impressions of one of the other pictures – *which was still in its sealed envelope* (below). No one was 'sending' it, so how did it happen?

Absent-minded

Dr Kit Pedler noted the curious phenomenon called the 'displacement effect' during remote viewing experiments at SRI (see page 39). But bypassing the actual target and homing in on one of the rejected targets instead is intriguingly common in other ESP experiments. And such 'misses' are often more interesting than direct 'hits', although researchers frequently overlook them.

criticisms and, in turn, found much to criticise. They had, he asserted, jumped to as many conclusions as, in their opinion, had Puthoff and Targ. Marks and Kamman, said Morris, had overstepped the mark by juggling with incomplete or improperly understood data and had reached the wrong conclusions. Morris conceded that the SRI experiments had required tighter controls and that there had been some serious weaknesses in the methodology employed. But the debunkers seem, like so many debunkers of psychic matters, to have missed the point. Sloppy methodology is one thing, but does it totally invalidate the basic premise that different people, in different places, can somehow 'see' with each other's eyes, telepathically?

Nothing but the scripts

Still with the SRI judging routine – and its inherent weaknesses – in mind, Marks and Kamman countered, they say, by trying another version. In this they removed the cues from the SRI scripts, gave the judges the targets and analysed the matches, assessed on the basis of the transcript alone. But they came up with only chance results.

However, Dr Charles Tart, of the University of California, also took up the challenge. He combines the qualities of being a refreshingly positive parapsychologist with a reputation for employing strict controls in all his experiments. Having edited out all extraneous information and cues, he resubmitted the scripts to a judge who had previously been successful at matching free-response material, though not at SRI. This judge matched the scripts to the targets at *above* chance odds.

So, imperfect as they were, perhaps the SRI remote viewing trials did prove that there is a strange, telepathic ability that so far we have only glimpsed. Puthoff and Targ's enthusiastic claims that everyone can score a direct hit with remote viewing seems, at present, a little fanciful. Yet there is an increasing body of evidence that suggests very strongly that other psychic abilities – metal bending for example – *can be learned*. There is also mounting evidence in other areas of psychical research that a positive attitude to psi can actively encourage phenomena to occur.

So perhaps the Puthoff/Targ experiments should not be despised. True, no one else has been able to come up with the same high number of direct hits, but perhaps no one else has been enthusiastic enough to encourage such positive findings. And even if they were muddled and ended up, in themselves, proving nothing, they have inspired others to take up the challenge to discover the hidden powers of the human mind.

Psychokinesis – the power of the human mind to influence physical objects – proves an elusive phenomenon under laboratory conditions. Exasperatingly, this is one of the most fascinating aspects of psi. GUY LYON PLAYFAIR reports on the scientific findings

OF ALL THE PHENOMENA OF PSI – the name given by researchers to parapsychology – psychokinesis has proved the most difficult to pin down under experiment. The Oxford dictionary defines it as 'the movement of physical objects by mental influence without physical contact'; more simply, it is mind over matter. It manifests itself in many ways: the bending of pieces of metal, the movement of objects, the influencing of chemical processes such as the developing of photographic film and of biological substances like blood or body tissue, all without direct contact or any explanation in terms of orthodox physics.

Psychokinesis – PK for short – has a long

Phenomenal successes

history. It has engaged the attentions of scientists since at least the 17th century, when Sir Francis Bacon suggested using 'the motions of shuffling cards, or casting dice' as a way of testing what he described as 'the binding of thoughts'. (This is, of course, precisely what Dr J. B. Rhine did more than two centuries later, when he embarked upon his 50-year study of psychic phenomena under laboratory conditions.)

However, it was only after the birth of Spiritualism in the mid 19th century that serious attempts were made to find out exactly what was going on. In 1854 Count Agénor de Gasparin published an account of table-turning experiments in Switzerland, and concluded that the human will could act on matter at a distance. This opinion was supported the following year by Professor Marc Thury of the Academy of Geneva. The men reached their conclusions quite independently after thorough and extensive experiments with groups of friends, and neither thought it necessary to bring in the idea of 'spirits' to explain the workings of what they saw as a hitherto unrecognised force in nature.

At the same time, in the United States, Professor Robert Hare of Pennsylvania University set out to debunk what he called the 'popular madness' and 'gross delusion' of Spiritualism. But after a number of careful experiments using standard laboratory equipment – in one of them he recorded the exertion of a force equal to 18 pounds (8 kilograms) on an empty spring balance – he

changed his mind, and even became a Spiritualist himself.

In April 1870 two eminent parapsychologists embarked upon a series of 29 well-controlled and documented tests. One was the outstanding medium D.D. Home, and the other was William Crookes, one of the foremost scientists of his time, who had been made a Fellow of the Royal Society while still in his thirties for his discovery of the element thallium, and was later knighted. Crookes was soon fully convinced that Home was able to produce a variety of genuine PK effects, from rappings on tables and levitations of objects (including people, among them Mrs Crookes) to alterations in the weight of inert bodies. Many such effects were measured and recorded. There was, Crookes declared confidently, a new form of energy, which he called the *psychic force*, and he was one of the first to draw attention to the 'manifest relationship to certain psychological conditions' of what we now call PK – the fact that psychic abilities are closely linked to the state of mind of the subject. He also suggested that PK implied the existence of other dimensions, with the observer 'in infinitesimal and inexplicable contact with a plane of existence not his own.'

Later experiments gave Crookes's ideas considerable support, and many of his experiments with Home were repeated by several European scientists, including the Nobel laureate Charles Richet and the physicist Sir Oliver Lodge, with the Neapolitan medium Eusapia Palladino as subject. She

Left: a seance in progress. The moving glass is the closest thing to true psychokinesis that most people experience. On rare occasions the glass will move on its own for a few seconds, and true PK occurs

Below: a contemporary illustration of a table-turning seance conducted in Switzerland around 1853 by Count Agénor de Gasparin. His account of his experiments, published in 1854, was one of the first to suggest that the human will can act directly on matter

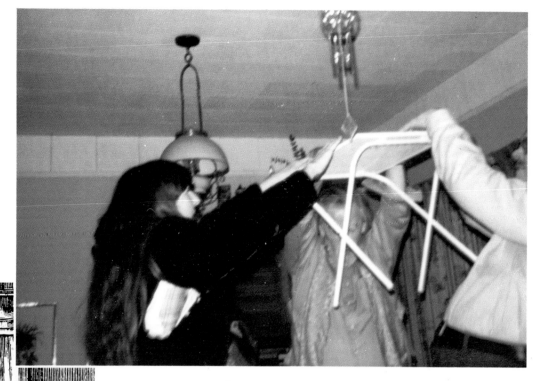

Above: members of the Society for Research into Rapport and Telekinesis (SORRAT) levitate a table. The SORRAT group became so good at inducing PK that such phenomena soon became regular occurrences at their meetings

Below: Alla Vinogradova caused a pen to move by PK, in an experiment filmed in Moscow. The USSR has produced many gifted physical mediums

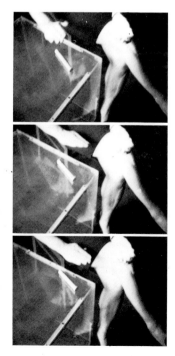

was studied intensively over more than two decades, most successfully by a three-man team from the British Society for Psychical Research, headed by the Hon. Everard Feilding, in 1908. Although Eusapia Palladino was not above faking 'paranormal' phenomena when she was unable to produce real ones, the team recorded a total of 470 events they were satisfied were truly inexplicable. In their 263-page report, one of the classics of psychical research, Feilding and his two colleagues – who, as well as being experienced psychical researchers, were also good amateur magicians – testified to their 'complete certainty' and 'absolute conviction' as to the genuineness of the phenomena.

It seemed that more evidence for the existence of PK was hardly necessary. But the case of a young Polish medium, Stanislawa Tomczyk, provided useful confirmation. She was carefully studied between 1912 and 1914 by a number of researchers, including Feilding (who later married her). He noted that, while she could produce poltergeist-like phenomena spontaneously and unexpectedly in her normal state, she could also produce them more or less to order under hypnosis, making spoons and matchboxes move around and even rise into the air just by placing her hands near them.

Thus, by the time Dr J. B. Rhine began his statistical analysis of PK in his laboratory at Duke University in North Carolina in 1934, there had already been published volumes of experimental evidence for its existence. Rather than amass still more evidence from the seance room, Rhine preferred to follow Bacon's suggestion and see if people could indeed 'bind' their thoughts to dice and influence the way in which they fell. After a series of rigorous experiments, using

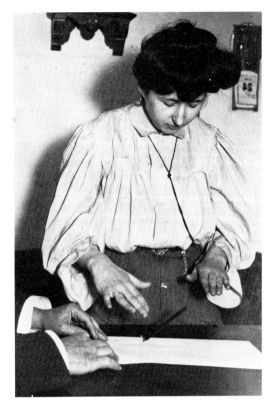

Left: Stanislawa Tomczyk, a Polish medium whose PK abilities were carefully studied between 1912 and 1914 by a number of psychical researchers. In a state of normal consciousness, she could produce spectacular poltergeist-like effects, but could not control them; under hypnosis, however, she could produce them to order

Below: the British medium Suzanne Padfield. The psychical researcher Benson Herbert (bottom) found that she was able to influence the strength of a beam of polarised light

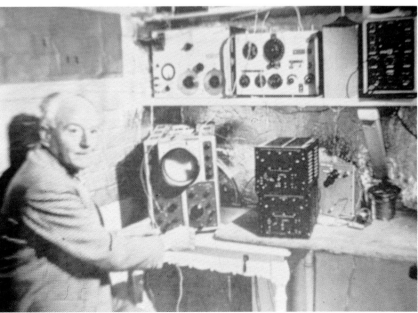

specially designed throwing machines to prevent any possibility of the subject being able to influence the outcome physically, Rhine was able to report that they could. His subjects – not people with any particular psychic ability, simply a more or less random selection of friends and students – recorded statistically significant results, sometimes against odds of millions to one. Towards the end of his career, Rhine stated his view that PK, like telepathy and clairvoyance, is an 'oft-repeated demonstrated experimental fact', and is an ability we all possess.

Mind power

Important as they were, Dr Rhine's findings left the world no wiser as to the mechanisms involved in PK. It seemed PK was produced by the influence of the human mind, and that certain paranormal phenomena that had previously been ascribed to other causes might also be susceptible of psychological – or parapsychological – explanations. In 1964 a British psychologist, Kenneth J. Batcheldor, set out with a group of trusted friends to try to reproduce the phenomena, using nothing more than positive thinking and considerable patience. If people really believed something could happen, he reasoned, then it would. And, sure enough, it did. In the course of 200 sittings, many of them recorded on tape, the group was able to produce many of the phenomena usually associated with the seance room – except that, in this case, no 'spirits' had been invoked. The table at which the group sat rapped in reply to questions, tilted in all directions, and repeatedly rose into the air even when somebody was sitting on it. On other occasions, it

would resist attempts to move it 'as if glued to the floor'. Cold breezes – a frequently reported feature of poltergeist cases – were felt, 'like standing in front of an open refrigerator', objects were thrown around the room by unknown means, and one sitter was dumped on the floor as his chair was pulled from under him 'as if by a steel hand.'

An interesting feature of Batcheldor's work, also reported by the Philip group in Toronto and the SORRAT researchers in the United States (see page 14) was that, although PK could certainly be produced to order, it tended to get out of control and manifest itself in the least expected ways, indicating either the action of some kind of subconscious force in the subjects, or the presence of independent entities – a possibility that seemed to lead right back to the controversial claims of the 19th-century Spiritualists. Whatever PK was, it was proving very elusive, and it came as a relief to researchers when physical mediums, who seemed to have disappeared from the scene altogether, suddenly began to reappear in the late 1960s. Here they had a more reliable source of PK phenomena.

The most important of these physical mediums is Nina Kulagina, a Leningrad woman born in the 1920s who became known to Western researchers in 1968. She is rare among psychics in being a powerful PK medium who co-operates fully with scientists and is able to produce effects to order roughly 80 per cent of the time. She has been filmed in action several times, and there is no evidence that she has ever used trickery. Benson Herbert, a British investigator, has called her 'the answer to a parapsychologist's prayer'.

She can make small objects move either towards or away from her on a table top, and can even cause three different articles to move in different directions at once. She has been observed stopping a pendulum and

Children and adolescents often have astonishing psychokinetic powers. June Knowles (left) can cause a plastic mobile to move inside a bell jar, while the young Californian psychic David Shepherd (below) specialises in bending metal

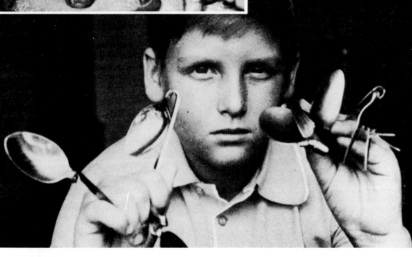

setting it swinging in a different plane. She has caused the downward movement of one pan of a scale while the other pan carried an extra weight. In addition, according to Dr G.A. Sergeyev, she has been able to stop the beating of a frog's heart and – even more alarming – to give a sceptical observer a heart attack.

Benson Herbert has good reason to believe in her powers. When she placed a hand on his forearm during a series of experiments held in a Leningrad hotel room in 1973, he felt unbearable heat. 'I think it possible,' he says, 'that if Kulagina had maintained her grip on my arm for half an hour or so, I would have followed the way of the frog.' Fortunately, like many PK mediums, she also appears to have some healing abilities, and has apparently managed to revive a dead fish in a tank.

After seeing a film of Kulagina in action, a New York medical technician named Felicia

Parise decided to see if she, too, could move things with her mind. After more than two months of hard practice, she succeeded, and was able to cause movement of a plastic bottle under the watchful lens of a film camera. Then, in one of her few laboratory experiments, she was asked to try to deflect the needle of a compass mounted inside an electronic metal detector and placed on a sealed packet of film. The needle swung through 15° and stopped, and would not move even when researchers Graham and Anita Watkins put a magnet near it. But when they removed the compass from the 'target area', the needle returned to north; when they put it back on the original spot, the needle again moved 15° and again resisted attempts to move it with the magnet. The film under the compass was found to be strongly exposed, though pieces of film at other nearby locations were only partly exposed, suggesting that Parise had created a localised magnetic field through mind-power alone – a field that remained for some minutes when she ceased to concentrate on it.

Psychic success

Parise might have become a second Kulagina, but she ended her brief career in PK in 1974, finding the work too much of a strain. In the same year, Matthew Manning began a three-year period of extensive laboratory PK tests before devoting himself to healing, and Benson Herbert published his work with another British medium, Suzanne Padfield, whom he found to be 'consistently successful' in influencing the intensity of a beam of polarised light. Meanwhile, in the USA, New York artist Ingo Swann performed a number of successful PK tests in different laboratories, including the alteration of the temperature registered by an electronic sensor, and the interference on the chart record of a shielded magnetometer. The metal-bending feats of the Israeli Uri Geller and the subjects of Professor John Hasted's experiment at Birkbeck College, London, England, are well-known; equally famous are the 'thought photographs' of the American Ted Serios. Advances in technology and research methods are, it seems, matched by the abilities of the PK mediums, to which no limit has yet been established.

'It staggers my imagination to conceive all the implications that follow now that it has been shown that the mind, by some means as unknown as the mind itself, has the ability directly to affect material operations in the world around it,' said Rhine, after a lifetime of study of PK and other psychic phenomena. 'Mind,' he concluded, 'is what the man in the street thought it was all along – something of a force in itself. . . .' The great challenge is to physics, biology and psychology: scientists must take PK into account if we are ever to reach a full understanding of the whole nature of Man and the astonishing powers of his mind.

Telepathy without tears

Sensory deprivation can be an instrument of torture, but in parapsychology it has provided the means for some remarkably successful experiments in telepathy.

THE SUBJECT LIES DOWN on a mattress on the floor of a quiet room in the psychology department of the University of Cambridge in England. Halved ping-pong balls are taped over his eyes, a red light is switched on a few feet above his head, and through the headphones he wears, an amplifier beams a steady stream of hissing, crackling 'white noise'. He is not about to be hypnotised – or tortured. He is in what psychologists call the *Ganzfeld* (German for 'whole field'), a state in which, though fully conscious and alert, he has been deprived of normal visual and auditory impressions. He is about to take

Bottom: throughout a Ganzfeld session the subject is bathed in a red light

Inset: subject Heidi Bartlet relaxes while Dr Sargent adjusts halved ping-pong balls over her eyes. These – and the red light – effectively block out all visual 'noise' (normal sensory stimulation), while Heidi listens to muted white noise through the headphones

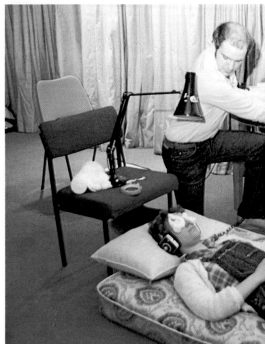

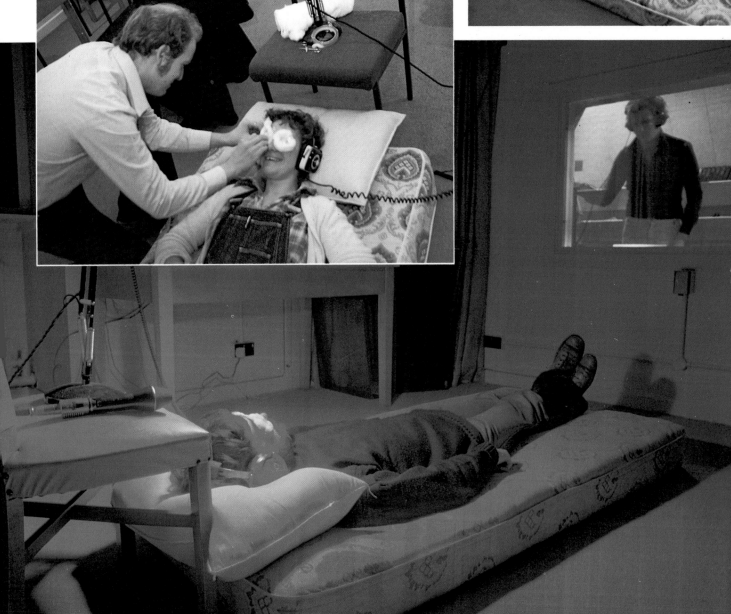

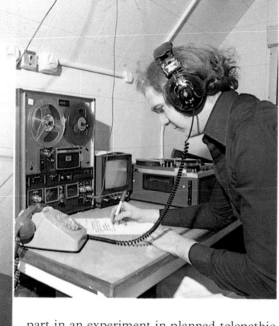

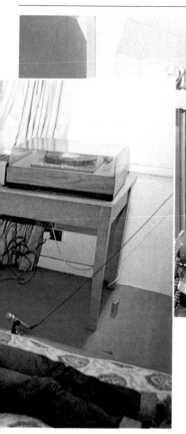

Above: Dr Sargent adjusts the level of white noise so that it blocks out all sound – while remaining comfortable for the subject

Above right: while the subject speaks her mental impressions into a microphone, Dr Sargent writes them down in the next door control room. Although her 'mentation' is taped, the written record is the basis for the later marking session

Right: a graph showing where Dr Sargent's subjects placed the target out of a pool of four pictures. By November 1981 there had been 458 experiments; out of these no less than 179 placed the target picture first, 114 placed it second, 93 third and 72 fourth. The 179 who were successful represent 39.08 per cent of the total number of experiments – the probability of getting such a high score is one in 100 million

part in an experiment in planned telepathic transmission.

'Our brains are programmed to respond to changing events,' explains Dr Carl Sargent, who is in charge of the Ganzfeld experiments at Cambridge. 'And if there is no change in our visual or auditory input, then maybe the brain will respond to the ESP channel.'

He clicks his stopwatch. 'Right,' he says, 'the experiment has begun.' In the adjoining control room, his assistant switches on a tape recorder and watches the subject through a one-way mirror. Then Sargent goes down the corridor to another room, sits down, and begins to stare at a picture, one of a set of four that has been selected for the occasion from 60 sets by a complex random process, so that neither he nor anyone else has any idea in advance what it will be.

Today's target picture is a landscape painting by the 19th-century Italian artist Giuseppi Palizzi. It shows a peaceful rural scene. In the foreground, an animal is being led towards the rustic house on the left, passing a large rock behind which there is a flat and barren landscape dominated by a large triangular-topped mountain, like a flattened pyramid, with a circular lake below it.

Sargent's task is to try to 'send' the contents of the picture into the mind of the subject in the other room. He focuses all his attention on the painting – its shape, colours and content – and he writes down some of the associations it has for him. 'Rather like the surface of the Moon,' he notes.

Meanwhile, the subject has settled down in his Ganzfeld environment. He finds it pleasant and relaxing, and soon, as instructed, he begins to speak into the microphone beside him, saying whatever occurs to him. After seven minutes, he says:

'Ah yes, there we go! Very clear. Dark animal standing on a rock, and a blue background. Mountain, blue – very clear, that.' A few minutes later, he adds: 'Looks more like

the detail of a rock now. Very clear.' And:

'Like a pyramid seen from the air – rocks – same as before. Like the top of Mount Everest or something. It's a very bleak landscape. . . . Big blob in the middle – perhaps it's the hole in the Earth?'

Finally, after 21 minutes in the Ganzfeld, the subject appears to score a direct hit:

'I'm still getting this desolate *Moon landscape.*'

Dipping into the pool

When the experiment ends, after about half an hour, the assistant comes in, helps the subject remove the ping-pong balls, and shows him a duplicate set of the four pictures from which the target was selected. At this stage, the assistant has no idea which one it was. She then goes through her notes, and asks the subject to match each statement he made to one or more of the pictures, scoring from 0 for no resemblance at all, to 99 for very strong resemblance.

The first picture is a news photograph of a naked undergraduate riding a bicycle along King's Parade in Cambridge. The second is a painting of some china ornaments and animals, the third is the Palizzi landscape, and the fourth is a cartoon by Heath Robinson showing an elderly couple rowing a boat.

The subject is confused. He immediately sees that the general shape and appearance of the cartoon are similar to those of the image he saw: the artist has drawn the white waves in such a way as to suggest a jagged lunar landscape, and the boat is roughly the shape of the rock he described. But there are several elements in the Palizzi that correspond to his impressions, and the second picture shows a china animal standing on a rock against a blue background. He seems to have picked up certain features of three of the four pictures, but when his scores are added up, the cartoon comes first and the Palizzi second, the china ornaments third and the naked student last.

Sargent now comes into the room and

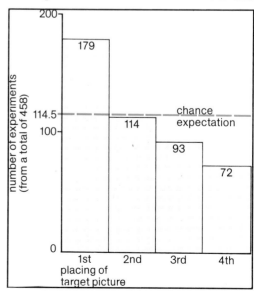

evening, with Sargent 'sending' a picture from his Cambridge home to the subject in London. It was agreed that the session would begin at 11.45 p.m., and for half an hour the subject, lying in his darkened bedroom with his eyes closed, received no impression at all. Then, 35 minutes after Sargent had actually stopped trying to transmit, the subject had a clear vision of a figure standing on a pedestal with a bright light behind it. After trying for a further 10 minutes, he saw the same image again, and then went to sleep, after jotting down his impression. Later, he learned that the picture Sargent had been concentrating on was Blake's *Glad day* – which shows a figure standing on a rock with a bright light behind it. Another coincidence?

Some successful subjects have described their target picture in uncannily precise

shows the subject his notes and the correct target picture. With hindsight, the subject wonders why he did not choose the Palizzi, and is impressed by the fact that both he and Sargent should refer specifically to a Moon landscape.

This single experiment proves nothing. Chance alone would predict that the subject should, at the end of the experiment, pick the correct target out of the target pool once every four times, giving a success rate of 25 per cent. But by the end of April 1981, after running a total of 412 sessions involving 146 different subjects, Sargent had come up with results that are very difficult to ascribe to chance alone. In these sessions, 37.9 per cent of first choices have been correct, and the percentages of rating the target picture respectively second, third and fourth have been 25.2, 20.4 and 16.5. In other words, there have been over 50 per cent more correct first choices than chance should predict. That this is due to consistently successful guesswork is statistically highly improbable. It is also of interest that almost twice as many first- or second-choice guesses as third or fourth have been correct.

In one series of experiments, Sargent set out to see if previously successful subjects would do better than previously unsuccessful ones. They certainly did. While the latter group scored 27.3 per cent correct first choices, almost exactly what they could be expected to score by chance or guesswork, the former achieved a hit rate of 83 per cent, a figure that could be attributed to guesswork only six times in 100,000. Successful Ganzfeld subjects, it seems, are likely to become more successful. In other words, *telepathic receptivity can be learned.*

The subject who had failed to score a correct first choice in the experiment described above decided to see if he, too, could improve – straight away. At his suggestion, he and Sargent held a test session later that

Top: Heidi Bartlet chooses the correct target picture out of the pool of four. Dr Sargent has discovered that Ganzfeld subjects can *learn* to get direct 'hits' consistently

Above: the scene by the 19th-century Italian artist Giuseppi Palizzi, which was the target picture in one notable experiment. Dr Sargent, who was the 'sender', noted down the phrase 'rather like the surface of the Moon'. The subject remarked during his mentation period, 'I'm still getting this desolate Moon landscape.' Coincidence?

detail. Hugh Ashton, one of Carl Sargent's regular collaborators, remarked during a test with himself as subject: 'I keep thinking of firemen and a fire station.' The target picture was of firemen in training at a fire station, and Ashton even mentioned that one fireman had his face towards the camera, a detail Sargent had not consciously noticed while transmitting. Such incidents raise the question of whether the sender is in fact sending by telepathy or the subject is receiving his impressions by clairvoyance.

There is even evidence for some unexpected precognitive side-effects in Ganzfeld studies. A Dutch journalist dreamed the night before his test that the target would be a surrealistic painting by Magritte. It turned out to be a Dali – the only surrealist work in Sargent's entire pool of pictures. Writer Roy Stemman made a correct first choice on his first attempt, but also reported images of Spanish dancers and a Mayan temple, which had nothing to do with the target. He then went home, switched on his television and found himself looking at Spanish-style dancing in a film about Mexico.

The original idea for Ganzfeld research

came from US parapsychologist Charles Honorton, while he was at the Maimonides Medical Center in New York carrying out experiments in dream telepathy. He kept noticing that most reports of spontaneous telepathy over the previous century had come from people who were in a highly relaxed state at the time, whether asleep, convalescing, or just doing nothing in particular. Therefore, he reasoned, instead of making people sit and guess ESP Zener cards *ad nauseam*, why not try to recreate the conditions under which telepathy seemed to happen in real life?

Alert – but dreaming

Attempts to transmit images to dreamers were highly successful, he found, but they took far too long. All night, in fact. He considered that the Ganzfeld environment was an analogue of the dream state, and that by placing somebody in it he would be creating an environment in which psychic experience could be expected to flourish, as indeed it did. By 1977, Honorton was able to report that not only had his own eight experiments, involving a total of 267 sessions, given significant positive results, but that 10 other researchers had been able to repeat them just as successfully or more so, to a degree he described as 'highly significant by the most conservative estimate'.

Carl Sargent makes no secret of his enthusiasm for his Ganzfeld work, which he first tried, with himself as subject, on a visit to Honorton's laboratory in 1978. 'It had a very powerful effect on me psychologically,' he says. 'I found it really did produce an altered state of consciousness, and I even had an incipient out-of-the-body experience.'

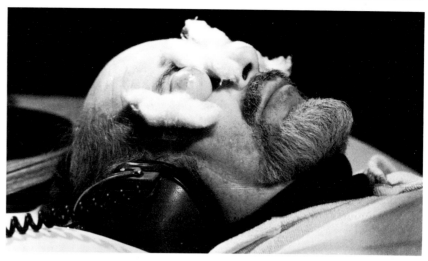

Top: the late Dr Kit Pedler taking part in a Cambridge Ganzfeld experiment

Above: Charles Honorton, the US parapsychologist who discovered the efficacy of the Ganzfeld

Left: *Glad day* by William Blake. This was a target that the subject failed to place first – but successfully picked up during a long-distance telepathy experiment that night

Subsequently, he achieved considerable success both as subject and as sender, and has found, by studying the psychological questionnaires he gives all his subjects, that extroverted types are far more likely to be successful than introverts.

He himself is the most exuberant of extroverts. 'Ganzfeld work is, above all, tremendous fun,' he says. 'People really enjoy it, and they keep coming back for more.' Yet however much he enjoys his work, he takes it very seriously. As the first person to be awarded a Ph.D. for a thesis on a parapsychological topic, and as a full-time parapsychologist (of whom in 1981 there were only about half a dozen in the whole of Britain, and probably not more than 30 in the West), he is well aware of the need to achieve scientific respectability if his subject is to attract the attention of other scientists and to encourage funding. Thanks to him, parapsychology became part of the syllabus for Cambridge undergraduates, and by 1981 eight of them had volunteered to undergo training in it.

Ganzfeld research is one of the most promising fields of parapsychology to have emerged since the metal bending of the mid 1970s, and it offers considerable promise for at least two reasons:

First, it has produced a very consistent and high repeatability rate, and second, it is largely fraud-proof, as there is no opportunity for the subject to cheat – deliberately or subliminally. It is also a clear example of a parapsychological hypothesis being put to the test and successfully repeated elsewhere, a standard requirement of any branch of science.

Moreover, unlike metal bending, it is of practical value in itself. Not only is it enjoyable and relaxing for most subjects, but regular practitioners have found it gives them an overall increase in sensitivity and awareness. For the first time in more than a century of psychical research, it seems that 'paranormal' abilities can, given suitable conditions, be learned and produced to order in the laboratory.

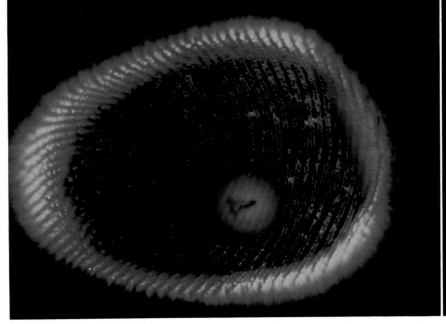

Images of the unseen

Do we have a spiritual body that exists separately from our physical body? For centuries mystics and clairvoyants have claimed that there is a halo of brightly-coloured light surrounding the human body. Then, in 1970, news was received that Russian scientists had photographed this 'aura'. BRIAN SNELLGROVE reports on their revelations

IN 1939 A RUSSIAN engineer, Semyon Kirlian, was repairing an electro-therapy machine in a research laboratory in the Ukrainian town of Krasnodar. Accidentally he allowed his hand to move too close to a 'live' electrode. The shock he received was accompanied by a brilliant flash of light given off by a large spark of electricity. His curiosity aroused, Kirlian wondered what would happen if he placed a sheet of light sensitive material in the path of the spark. Placing his own hand behind a piece of light-sensitised paper, Kirlian found on developing the film strange streamer-like emanations surrounding the image of his fingertips. On closer inspection, Kirlian found that each emanation was seen to have a different radiation pattern.

Fascinated by his 'discovery', Kirlian set up a laboratory in his tiny two-roomed flat and spent all his spare time investigating this phenomenon. Kirlian's research into high-voltage photography over the next 40 years led to intense scientific speculation and debate, and the claim, by some, that the strange emanations captured on film by Kirlian were proof of the existence of the so-called 'astral body'.

For centuries mystics and clairvoyants had claimed that they were able to see a brilliant halo of light surrounding the physical body of all living organisms. This 'halo', they believed, was the spiritual 'double' of our physical selves, but independent of it and surviving the death of the body.

Was the image that Kirlian was able to photograph that of the 'astral body'? Some have believed so. But at present it is not at all clear what causes the brilliant glow surrounding the hands, feet, plant leaves and other objects that have been photographed using the Kirlian technique.

Nor indeed were the effects that Kirlian thought he had discovered entirely new or unknown. In the 1890s, Nikola Tesla, a Serbian scientist working in the USA, had

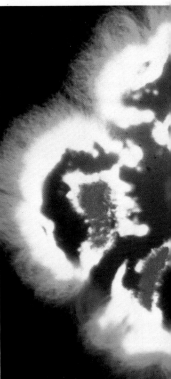

Top left: a fingertip photographed by the Kirlian method, which shows the surrounding radiation pattern. The vivid colour is not in fact significant. The colour of the aura tends to vary according to the type of film used: in this case, it is Ektachrome

Left: Semyon and Valentina Kirlian, the husband and wife team who spent over 40 years developing a technique to capture on film the strange streamer-like emanations that, in varying degrees of strength, surround almost all objects

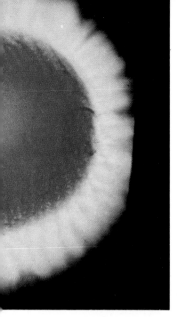

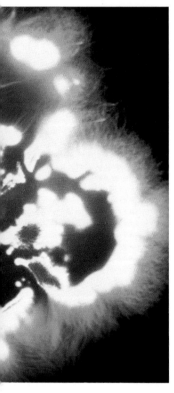

An amazing inventor

Born in Smiljan, Yugoslavia, 9 July 1856, Nikola Tesla became a driving force in the invention of electrical devices and equipment, as well as being something of a prophet.

Unable to interest European engineers in a new alternating current motor he had conceived, Tesla went to the United States in 1884 and joined Thomas Edison in the designing of dynamos. But the two men soon fell out. Tesla left his employ and set up his own laboratory dedicated to showing the feasibility of Alternating Current.

In 1891 Tesla unveiled his famous coil, which is still widely used today in electronic equipment, including television and radio. Tesla's coil is an electrical device for producing an intermittent source of high voltage. It consists of an induction coil with a central cylindrical core of soft iron onto which are wound two insulated coils: an inner (primary) coil of a few turns of copper wire, and a surrounding, secondary coil with a large number of turns of thin copper wire. An interrupter is used for making and breaking the current in the primary coil automatically. This current magnetises the iron core and produces a large magnetic field through the induction coil. For experimentation with the high voltage output of power from his coil, Tesla produced a gas-filled, phosphore coated tubular light – forerunner of today's fluorescent light.

A measure of Tesla's inventiveness can be seen by his tele-automatic boat of 1898 which was guided by remote control. Then in 1900 he made what many have claimed as his finest discovery – terrestrial stationary waves. He proved with this discovery that the earth could be used as a conductor and would be as responsive as a tuning fork to electrical vibrations of a certain pitch. He also lighted 200 electric lamps without wires from a distance of 25 miles and created man-made lightning, producing flashes of some 135 feet. Tesla was convinced at one time that he was receiving signals from another planet at his Colorado laboratory. But his claims were met with derision from the scientific press.

His ideas later became even more speculative. He asserted that he was able to split the world in half like an apple and that he had invented a 'death ray' that could destroy aircraft 250 miles away. His ideas concerning communication with other planets met with incredulity. Yet in 1917 he accurately forecast the coming of radar.

Top: a brilliantly illuminated Kirlian picture of a fingertip. A strong 'aura' is said to show ESP powers, sometimes latent, in the subject of the photograph

Above: as this picture of an oleander shows, plants also respond to the Kirlian method. This fact has been taken by some to prove that all life is essentially spiritual

used high-voltage photography, with much the same results as those achieved by Kirlian. In the early 1930s an English researcher, George de la Warr, discovered the existence of weak 'electromagnetic force fields' surrounding areas of the human body and at a distance from it. These fields extended in a lattice-like formation and contained voltage peaks as high as 70 millivolts. The vividness of these fields was also seen to fluctuate according to the physical and emotional state of the subject.

But undoubtedly the major advances in the field of high voltage photography were indeed made by Kirlian himself. Some of his most interesting contributions were made quite by chance. On one occasion, Kirlian was preparing his equipment for a demonstration he was giving to a distinguished visitor. To his dismay, on the day the visitor was to arrive the machine failed to produce the normal clear results. Kirlian took his machine apart, checked for faults and made further tests, but with the same negative results. In frustration he asked his wife, Valentina, to be the subject. To their mutual surprise, a perfect image was produced. A few hours later, Kirlian discovered what he believed to be the cause of his failure to produce a clear image. He developed a particularly virulent form of influenza, and to Kirlian it seemed reasonable to suppose that his illness had caused the weak image. The photograph, Kirlian claimed, had in some way given warning of the influenza.

A further possible use of the Kirlian method was revealed when the chairman of a major scientific research institution arrived. He brought with him two apparently identical leaves for the Kirlians to photograph, the

Controlling the Kirlian aura

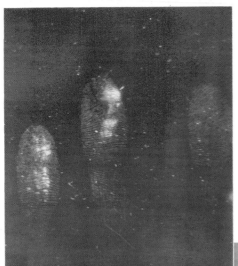

From the age of 11 Matthew Manning, below left, has been aware of possessing a wide range of psychic powers. Powers that he could, with practice, turn on at will. In 1974 a group of 21 scientists met to investigate these powers. Was Matthew being used by supernatural forces outside himself, or could his 'gift' be explained in terms of science? The evidence remains inconclusive. But Kirlian photographs taken of Matthew's fingertips produced startling results. The picture on the left shows Matthew's 'normal' corona, but the picture below, taken when he had 'switched the power on', shows a remarkably intense aura.

A Kirlian photograph of a rose petal (top right) shows a characteristic aura. But when a portion of the petal is cut away (below right) the Kirlian photograph still shows, quite clearly, the section that has been removed. This is known as the 'phantom leaf effect' and Russian investigators say that it proves that 'bioplasma' surrounds all living things

Below: a 50p coin with the characteristic outer 'glow'. If, as some claim, this glow is really the 'aura', then it would imply that even inanimate matter has some form of spiritual existence

Bottom: the same coin photographed after two psychic healers had placed their hands 4 inches (10 centimetres) above the coin for five minutes. The outer glow is noticeably brighter

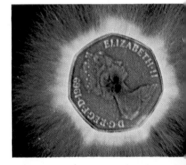

two samples had been taken from the same species of plant, torn off at the same time. From one leaf the husband and wife team obtained the characteristic flare patterns surrounding the leaf. But from the other leaf, no clear patterns were obtained. The Kirlians adjusted their machine in every possible way, but with the same inconsistent results. Next morning they related their failure to produce the same results to their visitor. To their surprise he was delighted. The leaf with the weak pattern, he told them, had been taken from a plant that had contracted a serious disease. The other leaf, with the clear pattern, had been taken from a perfectly healthy plant. The experiment seemed to confirm Kirlian's hypothesis: his machine was able to give warning of disease. The high voltage photograph had detected illness and disease in advance of any physical symptoms appearing on the surface.

Further experiments seemed to produce equally startling results. If a section of a leaf was cut off and photographed an image of the outline appeared on the photograph. This phenomenon, known as the 'phantom leaf', seemed to confirm the claims of clairvoyants that they could see clearly the 'phantom limb' on people with an amputated limb, but who continued to feel pain from the severed limb.

Though the Kirlians themselves did not describe the results of their investigations as evidence for the existence of an 'astral body', many were only too eager to do so. What other explanation was there, they asked, for the startling pictures Kirlian was able to take? But in one sense even the clairvoyants were disappointed with the results of Kirlian photography. Even the richly colourful images achieved by Kirlian lacked the subtlety of the 'aura' seen by clairvoyants.

While working at St Thomas's Hospital in London at the turn of the century, Dr Walter Kilner found that if he observed his patients through a glass screen coated with a blue dye,

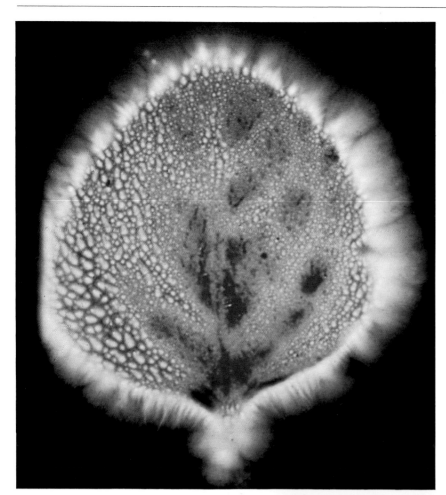

but also a counterpart body of energy'.

Much evidence already exists, claim the enthusiasts, to support Inyushin's theory. And there is also evidence that the nature and extent of these fields of energy, surrounding every living organism, corresponds to the image on the Kirlian print. Not so, reply the critics. Kirlian photography cannot be considered of scientific interest, since it is not repeatable under stringent laboratory conditions; a necessary requirement of all scientific phenomenon. Also, they argue, those experiments that have been conducted produce different results every time, not as the result of underlying physical or psychological causes, as Kirlian claimed, but due, simply, to such factors as sweat secretion and the primitive nature of the equipment used in Kirlian photography.

The debate continues. No one knows for certain what the images the Kirlians photographed are. Some, while rejecting the spiritual aspects of Kirlian, accept that, whatever the emanations mean, they can be used to achieve insight into the physical and psychological condition of the subject. Others, including practising scientists, claim far more. But all are agreed that the Kirlians have opened up a hitherto invisible world, once known only by the exceptional few, for everyone to see.

he could see a 'faint cloud' surrounding them that seemed to vary according to the physical and mental state of the patient. The dye had, Kilner later came to believe, acted as a stimulant to his own innate ability to perceive the 'glow' without any artificial aid. But the ability of those like Kilner to see this 'aura' clearly is of little help to scientists. Because it is such a personal quality, it is difficult to measure, control, analyse and subject to scientific scrutiny in the laboratory.

Research in the West into the possible cause of Kirlian photography is still in its infancy. Certainly, no definite conclusions have been reached. Research in Russia has been of much longer duration and has contributed many interesting theories as to the possible cause of the Kirlian effect. Working at the University of Alma Ata, Dr Viktor Inyushin has spent several years investigating Kirlian photography. As a result of his investigations, Inyushin has come to the conclusion that the 'aura' effect shown in Kirlian photography is evidence of what he calls 'biological plasma' and not the result of any electrical state of the organism. Dr Inyushin describes 'biological plasma' in terms that closely resemble those used by clairvoyants to describe the 'astral body'. 'All living things' writes Dr Inyushin '– plants, animals and humans – not only have a physical body made of atoms and molecules,

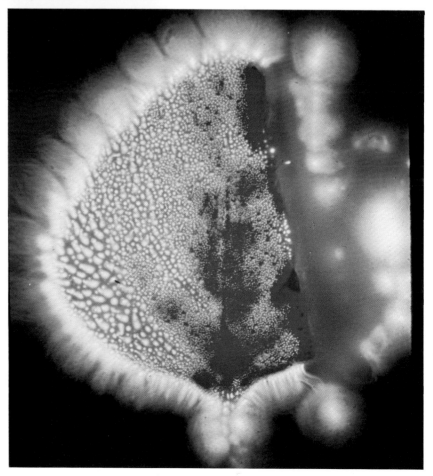

Reading between the lines

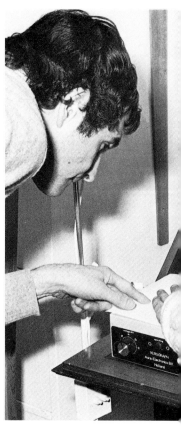

Left: the bright glow surrounding this gold cross is attributed to the influence of the wearer's 'aura'. Gold is able to retain the 'aura' indefinitely

Above: the author, Brian Snellgrove (left), operating a Kirlian machine. The regularity of the corona produced by the subject's hand can provide information about his personality and state of health

Can Kirlian photographs reveal the early stages of cancer? Does a disturbed 'corona' indicate stress and anxiety? What else can Kirlian photography detect?

WHEN RUSSIAN SCIENTISTS announced the discovery of an 'energy body' composed of 'bioplasma' existing quite separately from the physical body, few scientists in the West were prepared to take them seriously. What evidence was there, they asked, to substantiate such a claim?

And the question, despite much scientific investigation, still awaits a conclusive answer. What the Russians believed to be the 'energy body' turned out to be the curious corona shown by Kirlian photography to surround almost all living things. But, as sceptics in the West asked: what exactly is the strange corona effect that Kirlian photography is able to capture on film? Does it really constitute, as some have claimed, positive scientific evidence for the existence of an 'energy body'? Is the corona effect, perhaps, a picture of the 'aura' that has been described by mystics and clairvoyants? Or is there some

other, perfectly ordinary, explanation?

Recent research has been concerned to show that whatever Kirlian photographs may mean, they can be used to achieve practical benefits in medical diagnosis and insights into the human mind. For example, a relationship has been found to exist between the various patterns of Kirlian photographs of the human hand and the physical and psychological condition of the subject.

The left hemisphere of the brain corresponds to the right hand, and radiations from it detected by Kirlian photography provide clues to the logical ability of the subject. The intuitive potential of the subject can also be discovered by a reading of the corona effect of the left hand, which correlates with the right hemisphere of the brain. Both hands in a state of balance show a well-balanced personality.

Characteristics that can be recognised by

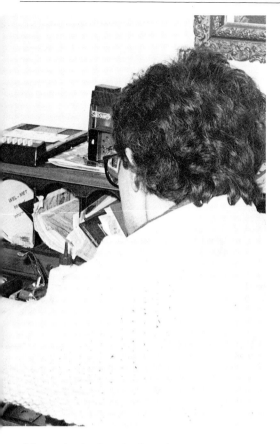

this method of analysis – characteristics that the subject himself may not realise he possesses – include healing ability, creative potential and qualities of leadership. Kirlian photographs are also said to show the nature and extent of conflicts arising from professional and emotional life and also the existence of physical tension.

Initial investigations into the diagnostic possibilities of Kirlian photography have revealed a wide range of possibilities. Studies on rats carried out by Dr Thelma Moss and Dr Margaret Armstrong of the University of Rochester, New York, indicate that marked changes occur in the corona discharge of the tails of cancerous rats as compared to those of non-cancerous rats. Similar corona patterns have been found in cancerous plants and in the fingertips of cancerous humans. Virtually all areas of the body photographed by the Kirlian method have yielded some information about the physical and mental condition of the subject. However, areas where the clearest corona pictures are obtained are the hands and feet.

The basic equipment used in Kirlian photography is simple, and consists of a high voltage 'Tesla coil', which is connected to a metal plate, and which is insulated from the subject by a non-conductive layer. A sheet of light-sensitive material – bromide paper or film, for example – is placed between subject and machine.

The Kirlian machine radiates a high-voltage, high-frequency field. The 'energy body' of the hand or object to be photographed repels the field and causes a pattern of interference to be established. This 'energy body', or whatever it is that creates the pattern, varies. When the 'energy body' is in a balanced condition a regular interference pattern is produced when the field of the machine and that of the subject interact. When there is an imbalance in the field of the subject, irregularities appear in the corona. And it is these irregularities, as research has shown, that can often be correlated to some physical or mental ailment.

Energy of the soul?

Despite the quite beneficial results that have been achieved, Kirlian photography is still beset with many theoretical and practical difficulties. Perhaps the most controversial area of Kirlian photography centres on the interpretation of results.

There are at present four broad views taken of Kirlian photography. According to the cynical view, the so-called Kirlian effect is merely the result of normal discharge between the subject, film and the machine. Any accurate diagnosis produced is purely coincidental and is due solely to the intuition of the researcher. Accepting that Kirlian photography can monitor physical symptoms such as the activity of the sweat glands and temperature, more sympathetic critics say that it still needs to be shown that these changes reflect changes in the physical or psychological state of the subject before proper diagnosis can be made.

Parapsychologists, however, insist that although purely physical causes, such as sweat, may play a part in the production of

Above: a Kirlian picture of a slice of wholewheat bread. Russian experts on nutrition are said to have used the Kirlian process in improving the quality of grain and other foodstuffs

Right: a photograph of a healthy geranium leaf taken with a conventional camera

Far right: the same leaf photographed by the Kirlian method. The corona surrounding the body of the leaf can be seen quite clearly

Below right: a Kirlian photograph of the same geranium leaf taken after the leaf has died. The corona effect has almost completely disappeared, leaving only the image of the leaf

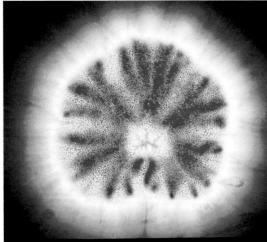

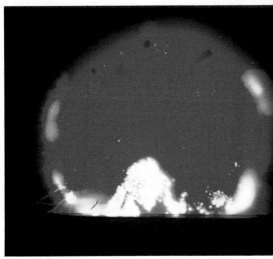

Below: the strong corona surrounding the foot of this subject suggests good health. But notice the absence of the corona around the big toe. This indicates that the subject is suffering from a headache. By massaging the toe, it is claimed, the headache will be eased

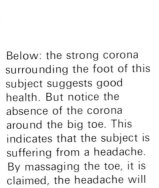

the corona effect, these causes by themselves do not provide a full explanation. According to parapsychologists, Kirlian photography can only be fully understood if the existence of an 'energy body', 'aura', 'bioplasmic body' or some other 'paranormal' phenomenon is accepted.

The most radical interpretation is that of the 'enthusiast' who claims that Kirlian photography has nothing to do with such mundane physical causes such as sweat. It shows, quite clearly, the energies of the soul. The colours and shapes revealed by Kirlian photography are what mystics and clairvoyants have been talking about for centuries.

Before being able to say which of these four competing views is most likely to be correct, there are a number of factors that the serious researcher has to take into account. The Kirlian machine used must conform to a certain standard to ensure that skin resistance, sweat, and other physical manifestations do not interfere with the corona. The subject being investigated must be relaxed. It has been found that when the majority of people try consciously to project their 'aura', the result is a weaker and more

irregular radiation. A similar effect is caused by anxiety or fear on the part of the subject. But, on the other hand, the researcher must be experienced enough to be able to distinguish between cases where the result is caused by anxiety, sweat, or some other temporary physical manifestation owing to nervousness, and those effects that indicate deeper physical or psychological significance.

There are, in addition, six areas where the Kirlian photographer needs to exercise caution if he is to avoid the more common criticisms levelled against Kirlian photography.

The area to be photographed needs to be chosen with care. A fingertip when photographed alone presents a different image from that of the finger when photographed as part of the hand. When photographing a single fingertip only the most acute abnormalities show up, so fingertip photography does have a limited usefulness in medical diagnosis. But for psychological diagnosis the larger the area photographed, the better the diagnosis.

There is a temptation to correlate the colours of the corona with an emotional state. The colour cast, however, depends solely on the type of film used. Ektakrome 35 mm film, for example, produces reds or yellows, while

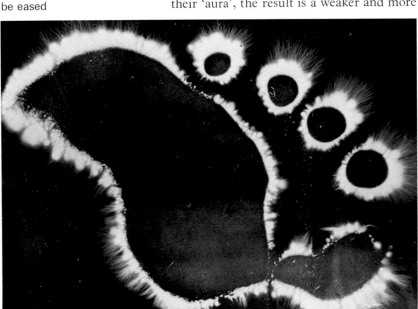

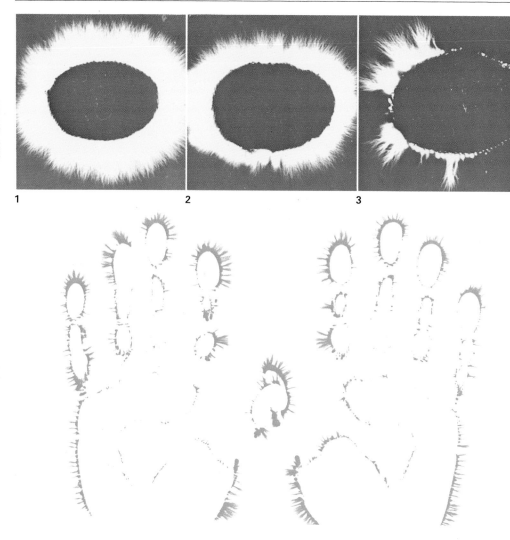

1   2   3   4

Above: a series of four Kirlian photographs of the same fingertips, taken at different times of the day. 1: 9.15 a.m., just after breakfast. Note the strong corona. 2: at 12.30 p.m., before lunch – the corona is noticeably weaker. 3: by 3.45 p.m., after only a sandwich for lunch, the subject's corona has faded considerably. 4: at 7 p.m., before dinner

Left: the 'spiky' nature of the streamers surrounding these hands is typical of tense subjects and indicates a lack of emotional flow. A well-balanced personality, on the other hand, has a softer, more regular corona

Polaroid film produces a red outer corona with a white inner band. Resin-coated paper produces blue and little else. The colours themselves are not important. What is important is the regularity and extent of any colour effects and what stimuli causes them.

Operator effect also needs to be taken into account. The ability of the mind to cause structural and emotional changes in both living and inanimate objects has been observed on many occasions. An aggressive attitude on the part of observers can inhibit the performance of ESP subjects; voltage patterns of wired-up plants change when disharmonious thoughts are projected. In order to exclude any possible effect of this nature, the operator should stand at least 4 feet (1.5 metres) away from the subject in a relaxed and open frame of mind.

Excessive voltage produces an artificially bright corona and the researcher needs to be able to recognise voltage and waveform characteristics. The golden rule is to use the minimum voltage required to produce a readable pattern.

The energy body takes time – sometimes a matter of days – to settle down after therapy. Results can also be misleading when photographing a subject after, for example, a session of meditation. In many cases the corona will have completely disappeared.

Too long or too short an exposure time can also produce misleading results. There appear to be slow cycles of activity that can be missed if exposure time is too short. For fingertip photographs, one second is sufficient; for the whole hand, two seconds.

In recent years Kirlian photography has been used successfully in a number of applications. In a study commissioned by a commercial firm in the USA, for example, Dr Thelma Moss was able to predict the incidence of germination of soya bean seeds with almost 100 per cent accuracy. The implications for agriculture are immense. Other areas where Kirlian methods of interpretation might be used include personnel selection and evaluation by employers of prospective employees, compatibility assessment and the estimation of the effect of parental conflict, particularly on children. When used in conjunction with acupuncture, counselling or homeopathy, Kirlian photography can produce accurate medical diagnoses.

While the practical benefits of Kirlian photography have been clearly shown, doubt remains as to whether it proves the existence of the 'aura'. There seems to be a 'flow of energy' surrounding almost all living things. But *what* that energy is remains unknown.

A crack in Kirlian's halo

Its champions claim that Kirlian photography can reveal a subject's character, emotional state, medical condition – even his very soul. But, says A.J. ELLISON, there is very little about the process that is strictly paranormal

IN THE MID 1960s I received from an academic staff member at a certain university a set of photographs – so-called Kirlian photographs. One was of a freshly cut leaf, the second was of the leaf after a piece had been cut out of it, the third was of a dead leaf. He told me how the photographs had been produced – in the way now known as Kirlian photography. His accompanying letter referred to the pattern of 'vital forces' shown by the bright tracks, spots of light and radiation surrounding the living leaf, the shadowy signs of an 'etheric body' of the part of the leaf that had been cut off, and the complete loss of all life and fire of the dead leaf, all the 'vital forces' having disappeared with death. He asked me, as an electrical engineer having some familiarity with high voltage discharge phenomena, and also as a Theosophist having a background of many years of study of etheric and astral bodies, of prana and such like, if I did not agree that the electric discharge was showing up remarkably clearly these 'subtle forces of life'.

I looked at the Kirlian photographs carefully, with an open mind. And the explanation seemed quite clear to me. As an independent check I consulted a colleague having a particularly distinguished reputation in the field of high voltage electrical discharge phenomena. It seemed quite clear to him too and we agreed. The differences between the photographs of the living and dead leaves were due entirely to the presence of the sap in the living leaf.

An 'etheric body' explained

But what of the etheric body of the cut leaf? The likeliest explanation of this was that the electrodes had not been carefully cleaned between the taking of the two photographs of the whole and cut leaf. So I looked (the opportunity occurred later) for evidence of this. A competent experimenter would know that the electrodes had to be cleaned carefully between the taking of the two photographs to remove all traces left during the first exposure, and he would have referred in his report specifically to this careful cleaning and inspection of the electrodes. No such reference was to be found.

So we had a perfectly good explanation of the pictures, which agreed with the description of how they had been made. We also had reason to suspect the competence of the experimenter.

I replied to my academic colleague to the

Above: Arthur J. Ellison has had a distinguished career as a psychical researcher and as a scientist. The president of the Society for Psychical Research, he is professor of electronic and electrical engineering at the City University, London

Above right: a detail from Matthias Grünewald's 16th-century altar painting in Isenheim, Alsace, showing the Virgin Mary surrounded by a halo. Artists have long signified the holiness of saints by portraying them emitting a heavenly radiance, which has been identified with the human aura or 'etheric body'. Some sensitives are apparently able to see the human aura, and it has been claimed that the Kirlian photographic process captures it on film

Right: this Kirlian photograph shows a rose leaf from which a small section has been cut – yet its 'ghost' remains visible. This has been described as scientific proof of a non-physical dimension to life – but the appearance of the 'spirit' of the leaf is probably due to physical traces of the whole leaf on the electrodes

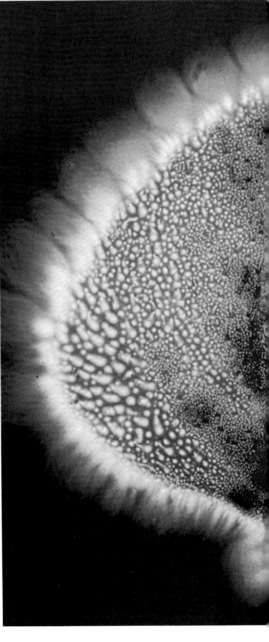

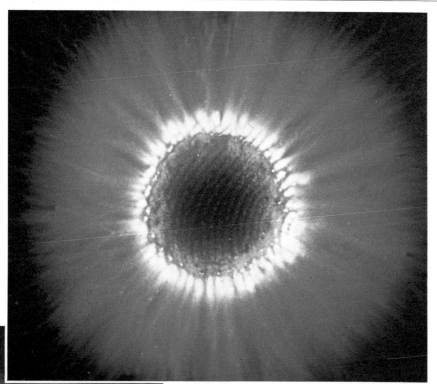

scientific method, either.

Most, if not all, writers on Kirlian photography, describing and evaluating their own 'researches' or those of others, are not competent to evaluate high voltage electrical discharges. Why should they be? This is a very specialised area of work involving a long professional training. It is clear why, to such writers, electric fields and discharges are just as mysterious as the etheric body is to the ordinary down-to-earth scientist who does not interest himself in such matters.

Further, such writers have not studied the scientific literature on the 'subtle bodies'. The term 'subtle body' is used by psychical researchers to describe bodies other than the physical body, which exist in a number of interpenetrating levels of consciousness. The first subtle body is the 'etheric' body, which – unrecognised by conventional science – is believed to carry 'life energies' of various kinds. It acts as a kind of bridge between the dense physical body and the more subtle astral body. Subtler still is the mental body, or mind; and there are supposed to be yet subtler bodies.

These subtle bodies are not made of some

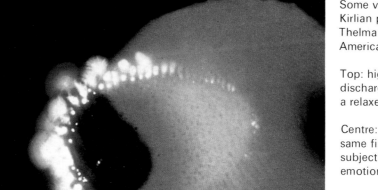

Some vivid examples of Kirlian photography made by Thelma Moss, a respected American researcher

Top: high frequency corona discharge from the finger of a relaxed person

Centre: photograph of the same finger of the same subject while under emotional stress

Below: fingertips of a subject who had taken marijuana

effect that in any further studies of Kirlian photography he would be well advised to seek the collaboration of a competent electrical engineer familiar with high voltage discharges. And I suggested that there was no need to involve 'subtle forces as yet unknown to science' until the normal explanations were exhausted. They were, of course, 'normal' only to an appropriately experienced electrical expert. To my colleague, who was not an electrical engineer, and to many others, the electrical phenomena were, and are, just as mysterious as the claimed 'occult' phenomena.

The perceptive reader of material on Kirlian photography will find that many writers on the subject have no knowledge of electrical engineering, even though high voltage discharges are the basis of Kirlian photography. Many have no knowledge of the

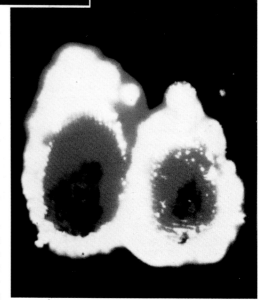

kind of 'subtle matter', which interpenetrates the physical body and projects all round. This is an entirely misguided way of looking at the matter. The subtle bodies are in 'other spaces', despite the fact that to the 'clairvoyance' of a psychic they do appear to interpenetrate the physical body.

A comparison might be made to 'waking dreaming'. The objects in the dream space are not to be considered as interpenetrating the physical world space and having position in it. This is quite easy for anyone to understand and has been shown clearly by experiments in which the position of someone's physical body has been screened while the psychic observed the etheric body. A psychic is unable to tell the position of the physical body by observation of a 'subtle body'. The experiments were carried out with the willing collaboration of some 20 experienced psychics and the results all agreed. It is most unlikely that there will ever be any physical way of making the etheric body visible to ordinary sight.

The unscientific writers also go wrong as a

Below: Kirlian apparatus employs this 'sandwich' arrangement. When an object such as a leaf is to be photographed, it is placed between the upper (earthed) plate and the film surface. When a fingertip, hand or some other part of the body is photographed, no upper electrode is required since the subject is, in normal conditions, earthed. If he is not properly earthed, however – perhaps because he has shoes with rubber soles, or is on a carpet with a rubber underlay – there may be a loss of quality in the Kirlian picture obtained

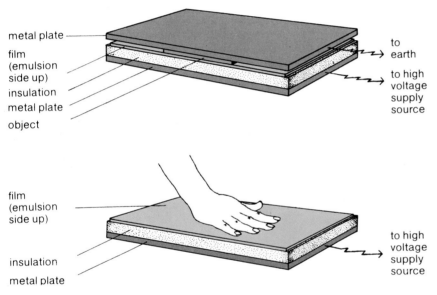

metal plate
film (emulsion side up)
insulation
metal plate
object

to earth
to high voltage supply source

film (emulsion side up)
insulation
metal plate

to high voltage supply source

result of not understanding how to apply the scientific method, especially how to remove from experiments, and their evaluation, the biases and preconceptions of the observer by using double-blind techniques. And they use *post hoc* reasoning: because a particularly dull picture happened to be followed by the illness of the subject, therefore the dullness was due to the incipient illness. They often select evidence that agrees with their preconceptions and ignore the rest. Some examples will illustrate mistakes listed above.

It is becoming quite common these days to get Kirlian photographs of fingertips or indeed of larger areas of the body. The Kirlian apparatus consists of a 'sandwich' made up of a flat metal electrode, a sheet of insulating material, a piece of colour film, and a second, earthed, electrode. In this case the finger is the second electrode, and is placed on the piece of film (emulsion side

Controlling the experiment

Dr Yoshiaki Omura proposes that these 24 points should be carefully specified in reports of Kirlian experiments:
1. High voltage frequency, measured at the power source and at the subject.
2. Oscilloscopic photograph showing waveform of the source.
3. Approximate range of output impedance of the source.
4. Approximate maximum voltage or voltage ranges, as well as waveform, polarities, duration, rise-and-fall time and repetition rate of the pulses.
5. Minimum and maximum distance between electrode plate and subject.
6. Details of the insulator between the electrode and the subject, with its size and geometrical arrangement.
7. Parameters of high voltage electrode plates (including shape, size and kind of metal and surface condition).
8. Name and characteristics of the film.
9. Electrode-to-film and specimen-to-film distances.
10. Exposure time for film and subject.

upwards), the sheet of insulation material below it forming the sandwich filling, with the metal plate below it connected to the high voltage supply source. The owner of the finger is at earth potential and the frequency is made sufficiently high so that he does not receive shock.

Some of the preceding chapters (see pages 52–55 and 56–59) showed several such fingertip pictures, some of which are claimed to indicate vibrant health (a bright discharge with lots of 'vital subtle forces flowing') and others to show illness or disease, real or potential, indicated by a very dull pattern of discharges. There were also photographs produced by psychics, first with the psychic doing nothing special, and second with the psychic 'force' switched on.

Important variables
Such claims involve comparisons among Kirlian pictures. A basic principle of the scientific method is that every variable except the one being compared must be the same, or at least controlled so that the effects of variations in these other variables are known. What variables are important as likely to influence the fingertip Kirlian picture when that picture is produced in the way described? Clearly, first the pressure of the finger. This would appear to be the most important variable of all, because the spaces under and around the finger and between the other members of the Kirlian 'sandwich' can crucially affect the form of the discharge.

11. Grounding conditions and approximate current through the subject.
12. Range of surface temperatures of the subject.
13. Electrical conductivity of the surface areas of the subject and the method used for measurement.
14. Whether (and how) the surface of the subject has been washed and cleaned.
15. Environmental conditions, including atmospheric pressure, room temperature, humidity, and degree of air pollution.
16. Pressure (approximate) exerted on the subject and the area of contact of subject with the surface of the film.
17. Vital signs (biological activity) before and after Kirlian photography.
18. Safety precautions.
19. Experimental set-up, shown in photographs or schematic diagram.
20. Voltage-current curves recorded by oscilloscope during photography.
21. Blood chemistry of subject.
22. Factors influencing circulatory conditions of various parts of the body.
23. Micro-circulatory states of the area of the body to be photographed.
24. Other pertinent information about subjects or procedure.

Other factors are clearly of importance too, such as the temperature, humidity of the air, voltage waveform and consistency, the duration of the discharge with its frequency, and the consistency of the film. There are, according to Professor Omura of the International Kirlian Research Association, 24 different variables that should be controlled. If at least the more important of these are not controlled then any comparison of Kirlian pictures is *meaningless*.

Some users of the Kirlian technique do not even measure and control the pressure of the subject's finger on the film. Their results are valueless and any deductions made from them are unlikely to be useful.

Let us take another example. Several years ago claims were made that, if a single Kirlian photograph were taken of the fingertips of two people who had not previously met, then each would show the 'normal' pattern; but if the experiment were repeated using two subjects who loved each other then their 'auras' (shown by the discharges) would be seen at least partially to merge. This claim was illustrated by striking Kirlian photographs. However, it would seem that the photographs had been selected from a large number of photographs that were not shown, probably because many of these did not show the desired effect.

Let us look at the way in which all the variables can be properly controlled so that pictures in which only one variable is changed can be compared. The controls should be checked by repeated photographs in which nothing has been changed: an artificial finger should be used with all the other variables unaltered. The photographs will then depend only on the type of film (the nature and distribution of the emulsions), the waveform and magnitude of the voltage, the thickness and material of the sandwich layers, and the number of discharges used on each occasion.

Reactions of the skin

When everything has been controlled and checked, the subject's finger may be placed on the pad. The changes in the picture will now depend on the physical/electrical parameters of the finger. The most important of these will be the electrical skin resistance, known to change with certain psychological variables, and the presence of sweat will clearly be a factor. Changes in electrical skin resistance are known to doctors and psychologists as the 'psychogalvanic skin reaction' or GSR. It will indicate changes in arousal, and it may also indicate the presence of disease. It can be changed by heavy breathing (resulting in over-oxygenation of the blood) and altered radically by deep relaxation, the skin resistance increasing greatly in a state of trance.

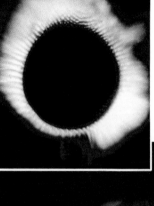

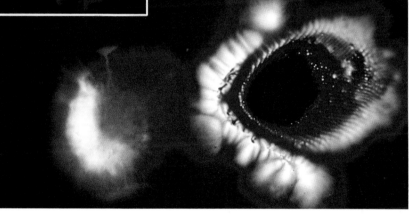

Above: fingertip Kirlian photographs obtained from a famous sensitive – Uri Geller. The upper picture shows the pattern obtained when Geller was at rest; the lower one, allegedly showing a burst of 'psychic energy', was taken after he had been invited to use his peculiar powers. What is perhaps more likely is that Geller, in concentrating, exerted extra pressure on his fingertips – or simply perspired more – and so altered the corona discharge around his finger

It is clear that properly controlled scientific experiments by competent people may well indicate that Kirlian photography has some diagnostic potential. But the emphasis has to be on proper control of the variables and sufficient experiments to be amenable to statistical evaluation, all human beings varying over a wide range in almost every respect. Such a study requires the collaboration of researchers from several disciplines – at least from electrical engineering and physiology – and is not easy. It has some possible value when carried out by trained people, but it is difficult to see any value at all in much of the material that is now being produced and published by experimenters who appear to have no qualifications to undertake such a difficult multi-faceted scientific study.

More than meets the untrained eye

Are all the claims made for Kirlian photography the result of exaggeration or wishful thinking?

IN THE PREVIOUS article I explained briefly how the 'etheric' body does not appear to be in physical space. This is a mysterious concept, and Kirlian experimenters propose to make the etheric body physically visible by means of something that, to those who are not electrical engineers, is equally mysterious – an electrical discharge. This is like trying to make the body you find yourself 'occupying' while dreaming visible to ordinary physical sight in a similar way.

There are, of course, 'force fields' around the human body. The body is an electro-chemical machine: electric currents flow through it and the body is surrounded by weak magnetic and electric fields. There are also temperature differences between the body and its surroundings, so it is surrounded by a radiating thermal field; this is the basis of medical diagnosis by thermography. The body is surrounded by a field of moving air, which is due to these temperature differences.

In addition there is a 'field' of small particles being continually thrown off the body surface. Perspiration appears on the skin and evaporates. This perspiration contains various chemical substances depending in kind and concentration on the body's metabolism and general health, which are major factors in determining the electrical resistance of the skin. The nature and quantity of these substances is affected by psychological states, and can change very rapidly; it

Right: a heat picture or 'thermograph' of the human body, which can be used in medical diagnosis. The cool parts show blue, the warmest white or yellow

Far right: the environmental chamber used at the Polyclinic Medical Center to ensure that variables are kept constant during the Kirlian process. Among the instruments are a barometer, thermistor, pulse detector, oscilloscope, hydrometer and a room thermometer

Bottom: human skin, shown at 5000 times life size. Each tiny crevice will affect the high voltage electrical field in a Kirlian photograph

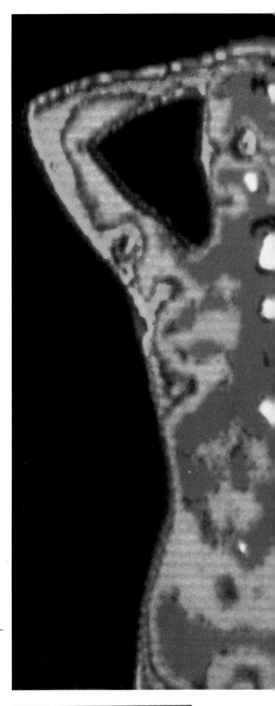

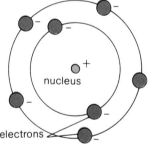

nucleus

electrons

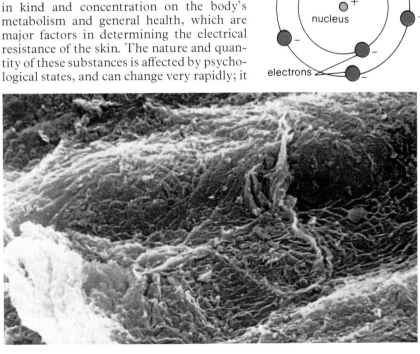

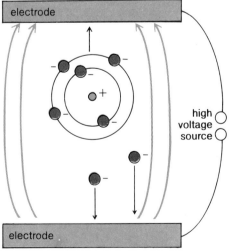

electrode

high voltage source

electrode

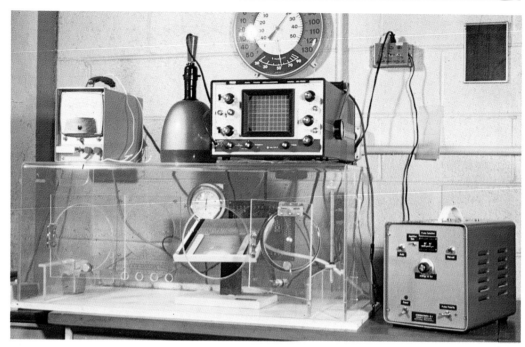

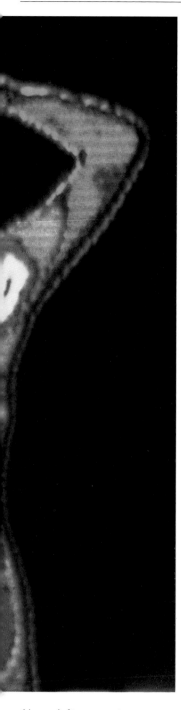

Above left: every atom consists of a nucleus around which electrons – particles of negative electricity – circle. Their charge balances the positive charge of the nucleus. A very intense electric field (left, shown by pink arrows) can pull electrons away from the atom. The free electrons and the incomplete atom are called ions, and move in opposite directions. In Kirlian photography, the ions create patterns when they strike the film. Though complex, the patterns are not mysterious

can also be affected by drugs.

Now let us look at what happens when an electrical discharge takes place between a finger pad and a high voltage electrode. The kind of glow produced in Kirlian photography is known as a corona discharge, and it is very different from a spark. Air is normally quite a good insulator, but if the voltage is sufficiently high the insulation may break down, and a single or continuous spark jumps the gap. When the current is small – as, for instance, in the spark produced by an induction coil – the spark can give one an intense shock, but it is not particularly harmful; on the other hand, a stroke of lightning, for example, carries very high current and is usually fatal.

Colour and form

The corona discharge occurs at lower strengths of electric field – that is, in essence, at lower voltages – than that required for spark breakdown, and it carries a low current; it is, therefore, harmless. It is caused by intermittent ionisation of the air around the fingertip, and it is therefore affected by irregularities in the electric field strength due to the ripples and folds and other irregularities of the skin. Other factors that will affect the nature of the corona include the nature of the insulating material between the finger and the plate, and the pressure and composition of the surrounding air.

The colours in the corona discharge result from the light produced by the ionisation of atoms and molecules, and the subsequent recombination of ions and electrons; and each substance will produce a characteristic colour. Everybody is familiar with the colour of a sodium discharge lamp or a mercury vapour light. Yellow is the characteristic discharge colour for sodium, and blue-violet for mercury. Air, which is made up of mostly

nitrogen and oxygen, normally has a blue-purple discharge corona; but a finger that is sweating heavily may well produce yellow streaks, since the sweat will be rich in sodium chloride, or salt.

The colour of the corona will also depend upon the variation of voltage with time, and upon whether the finger is the negative or positive pole of the discharge. And, finally, the nature of the photographic film used is also of importance. Colour film has three layers of emulsion, each of which will behave independently as part of the Kirlian 'sandwich': the current itself will directly affect the colours of the final picture, and the magnitude and distribution of this current will be affected by the nature and structure of the layers of film. It is quite clear that a photograph of the corona taken with a normal camera will be very different from the picture obtained on the film actually involved in the discharge process.

In scientific studies of the Kirlian discharge with so many different parameters, all affecting the result to varying degrees, it is necessary to keep all of them except one constant, so far as is possible, and then to vary that one and observe the effect.

It is a fact of some importance that the Tesla coil, used by so many investigators, produces a very unstable voltage supply, varying randomly in waveform and frequency. Serious scientific work needs a more controlled arrangement such as would be provided by an oscillator with an adjustable and stable frequency and fixed waveform. Differences in Kirlian photographs from eastern Europe and from the West, or between researchers in the West, are not surprising as there is as yet no standardisation of equipment: both the frequency and waveform – and also the time the discharge is passed for a photograph – vary according to

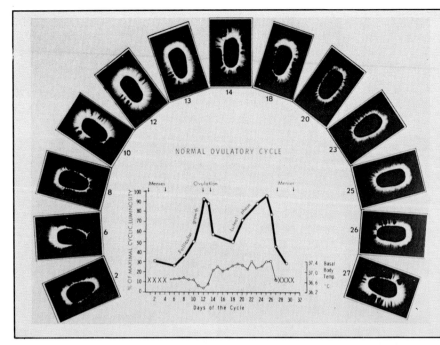

The fingertip test

Shown here are some results of the research into menstrual cycles conducted by Leonard W. Konikiewicz's team. On the left is a series of Kirlian images taken from a woman with a normal cycle; on the right they are from a woman taking Lo-Ovral birth control pills. The thick line on the graphs shows the relative luminosity of the Kirlian images, while the thin line on the left shows body temperature. There seems to be no correlation between the images and body temperature, but there *is* a relation between ovulation and the intensity of the corona; and the 'steady state' of the body, maintained as the pill prevents ovulation, is reflected in the consistent intensity of the Kirlian images in the set on the right.

the arrangement of the experiment.

Let us suppose that a suitable stable finger pad electric discharge has been produced and all other parameters kept appropriately constant and then comparisons are made between photographs of sick subjects before and after 'healing'. Should there be normal differences? Of course there should. 'Healing' most certainly affects the chemicals appearing in the sweat ducts – the primary cause of the large changes in electrical skin resistance when a subject becomes more tranquil and relaxed. Merely sitting quietly with someone's hands gently resting on one's forehead, particularly if it is accompanied by a belief that mysterious healing 'forces' are also flowing, will cause enormous changes in chemical secretion. If the comparison of Kirlian pictures before and after healing is confused by variations in an unstable electric supply source, in the finger pressure and ambient temperature and perhaps in the humidity, too, the comparison is well nigh worthless. Almost every comparison of Kirlian photographs available is quite invalid for these reasons.

Some researchers have noticed similarities between traditional eastern descriptions of the flow of 'prana' and 'vitality globules' and the appearance of 'bubbles' and stream lines in the corona discharge. The interchange of 'rose-coloured prana' between healthy and sick people has been suggested as a possible explanation of differences between finger pad Kirlian photographs of such people before and after healing. It would appear as yet to be far too early to take such similarities seriously.

So what should be done? Kirlian research requires a team involving, ideally, an electrical engineer, a psychologist, a physicist or chemist (expert in spectroscopy) and a physiologist. The experiments must involve

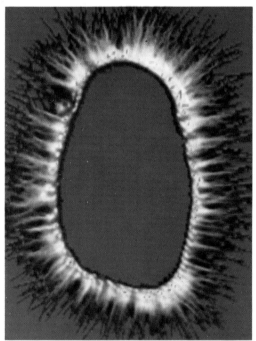

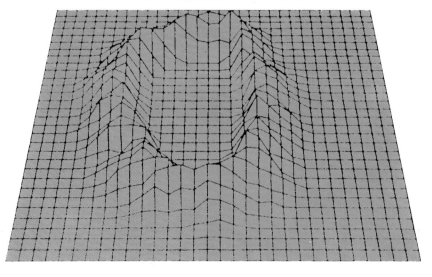

Top: two computer-processed Kirlian images show the difference between a healthy subject (left) and a patient suffering from cancer (right). Most cancer patients show a higher than usual light emission around the fingertips – marked here by the computer in red

Bottom: three-dimensional histograms made by computer analysis of Kirlian images. The control image above is thus seen as a regular series of 'bumps' (left), while a patient suffering from cystic fibrosis produces spikes on the graph (right). These correspond to high sweat emissions that show up brightly on the Kirlian image

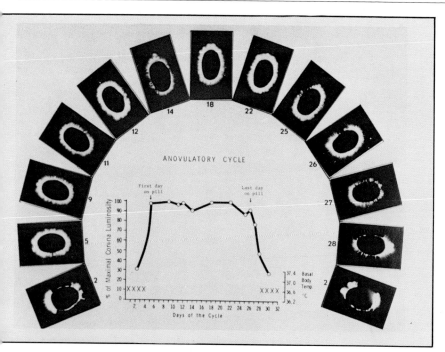

ANOVULATORY CYCLE

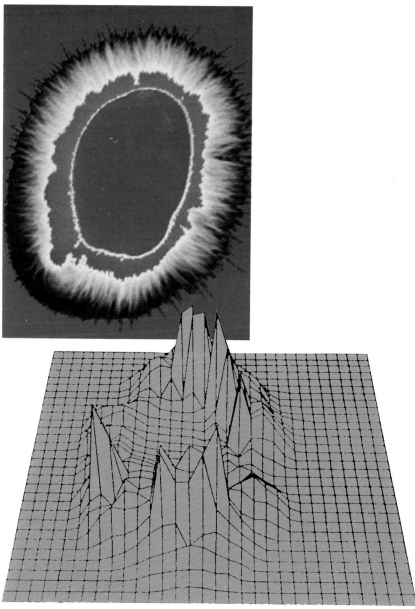

proper control of the parameters, double-blind comparisons, and a statistical evaluation, using a sufficient number of subjects and results from each. This research, as is the case with so many matters often considered parapsychological, *must* involve experts in many disciplines because no one person could be sufficiently expert in all the areas of knowledge involved.

The Objects of the International Kirlian Research Association of New York City seem to be on the soundly scientific lines needed to get to the bottom of this most interesting and perhaps very important phenomenon. Those lines are well exemplified by current work in the Polyclinic Medical Center, Harrisburg, Pennsylvania, USA, directed by Leonard W. Konikiewicz, who has produced a valuable book and a number of papers. In his work he uses all the controls referred to above, including an environmental chamber. He has verified the significance of a number of factors and discovered others previously unknown. For example, a rotary movement of the finger prior to exposure records a 'phantom image' by altering electron scattering.

Research makes the difference

Konikiewicz has found it essential to use special retainers to keep the film flat. Subjects must refrain from drugs and, two hours before tests, cleanse their thumbs with distilled water, dry them in air and then wear cotton gloves up to the test, to prevent contamination. In two blind studies involving 140 subjects, Konikiewicz correctly identified cystic fibrosis in 16 out of 18 CF patients and carriers of the gene in 37 out of 48. He could not differentiate controls from carriers if the relative humidity in his electrode environmental chamber (in which the hands are inserted through airtight openings) fell below 60 per cent, but he could still recognise CF patients. Earlier problems showed how the original Kirlian equipment (based on x-ray machine practice) with its very high frequency, stimulated the nerves controlling the sweat glands of the fingers – not always desirable. Konikiewicz solved these and other problems. Other work by this investigator shows, statistically of course, the variations in maximum luminosity of the corona discharge from finger pads of female subjects according to the day of the menstrual cycle. The day of ovulation, with other features, can be clearly seen. The patterns are quite different for subjects taking 'the pill' (see box).

It is clear, then, that while scrupulously conducted research like this may well vindicate the Kirlian process as a diagnostic tool, the information it provides is very much of *this* world and no other. Similarly, only research that maintains the highest professional standards will be of any use. The more widely these points are understood, the less likely it is that Kirlian's 'enthusiasts' will be able to mislead the uninformed.

Harry Price

Many years after his death, the flamboyant figure of Harry Price, psychical researcher and entrepeneur, continues to excite controversy. RENÉE HAYNES gives a new assessment of the varied career of this extraordinary man

HARRY PRICE IS FAMOUS for his work in bringing psychical research to the attention of the public. He was a man of a warm heart, a clear head, a keen nose for news – but his work was bedevilled by the fact that he also had much ambition, no academic conscience, and a passion for the limelight. In his autobiography *Search for truth* he recorded that in his youth he had wanted to become a writer; and he retained throughout his many books and articles a gift for producing lively and very readable material – too lively, too readable for some of his critics, who felt that he preferred a telling phrase to minute scientific accuracy. Among his ambitions were to contribute to *Encyclopaedia Britannica* (which his father, in Harry's childhood, bought in monthly instalments); to be in *Who's who*; to collect the largest library of books on magic in existence; and to be offered an honorary doctorate by a university.

In search of Harry Price

He succeeded in most of these aims. He did contribute to *Encyclopaedia Britannica*; he appeared in *Who's who* (though some of the statements he made in his entry were queried after his death). And he certainly amassed a huge library. After enquiring as an incredulous eight-year-old just how an entertainer had got two pigeons out of an empty hat, he was given a 'conjuring manual', the first item in what was to become a collection devoted to conjuring tricks, Spiritualist writings and objective psychical research. As far as his ambition to be awarded a degree *honoris causa* was concerned, a suggestion was indeed made that he should be awarded an honorary doctorate, by the University of Bonn, in consideration of his offer to co-operate in setting up a parapsychology department there in conjunction with Professor Hans Bender. Price withdrew in 1937, however, when he thought that the University of London might fund a similar venture – and the doctorate was not awarded.

According to Price's own account, his interest in psychical research started early. As a boy, he claimed, he spent much of his spare time wandering round street markets and fairs looking at fortune tellers, hypnotists, quack doctors, and conjurers, and closely observing their methods; and on occasion he visited local seances. He also began to write plays, to cultivate an interest in archaeology and to collect Roman coins. On leaving school he joined classes in electrical engineering, and later evening classes in mechanical engineering, chemistry and photography.

He wanted to become an engineer, but by the time of his marriage in 1908 he was, like his father before him, employed as a commercial traveller – a job that demands aptitudes for making new contacts, getting on with businessmen and sizing up situations quickly. It is interesting to compare Price's experience with his remarks in *Leaves from a psychist's case-book* (1933) on 'what constitutes an ideal psychical researcher'. To 'familiarity with psychic literature of all countries' he adds 'an acquaintance with foreign languages, a knowledge of chemistry, biology, physics, mechanics, medicine' – and conjuring. This formidable polymath must also have 'a charming personality, the hide of a rhinoceros, a clear conscience, a sense of humour, and exceptional tact'. Price himself certainly had a number of these qualifications – although many people would jib at describing his conscience in the matter of professional ethics in psychical research as clear. In fairness to him, it is only right to say that Price's undoubted talents lay elsewhere than in academic research. Energetic, ambitious, itching to make his mark in a world he had experienced as highly competitive, Price was in all probability unaware of the code of honour that many of his fellow psychical researchers took for granted professionally.

Above: Mrs K.M. Goldney, one of the distinguished members of the Society for Psychical Research with whom Harry Price co-operated in psychical investigations. Mrs Goldney was later one of the co-authors of *The Borley report*, which accused Price of fraud in his investigation of the poltergeist activity at Borley Rectory in Essex

Below: Harry Price addresses a meeting of the Ghost Club – dedicated to dining and discussion – which he resuscitated in 1938

Price's contrasting assumptions, his methods, and his undisguised love of publicity jarred upon them.

Sensitivity may make a man conscious that something is wrong, but it does not necessarily show what that something is. Price interpreted the chill disapproval of his colleagues in psychical research as social snobbery; this, understandably, aroused a deep resentment in him, and may well have led to the fantasies about his own ancient lineage and impressive professional background that he peddled as reality and that undoubtedly damaged his reputation for integrity.

Music hall turns

Price's marriage seems to have improved his finances – his wife had a small private income – and enabled him to spend more time on his overriding interest. During the years before the First World War he investigated both 'vaudeville mediums' appearing as music hall artists and small-time practitioners who gave private seances. He discovered that they relied on a fine assortment of tricks. One performer whose methods Price exposed insisted on using, wherever he went, his own armchair – which, he claimed, was 'saturated with magnetism'. Sitting in it in the dark, Price discovered, the 'psychic' could unlock a panel in the back against which he was leaning, and gain access to a collection of hairpieces, masks, rolls of butter muslin with coat-hangers to put them on, a collapsible dummy, and other props.

A heart ailment that troubled him all his

Above left: Harry Price as a young man, in a painting by J. Dumayne. After trying various careers, Price became a travelling salesman – a job that developed in him a quick-wittedness that was to stand him in good stead as a psychical researcher. This photograph (left) shows him demonstrating the electrical equipment he used to monitor the effects produced by mediums at seances

life prevented Price being called up for military service. Nevertheless, his knowledge of mechanical engineering meant that he was put in charge of a small munitions factory. He still had time enough left over from his activities there to investigate some 20 allegedly haunted houses, but with little definite result.

At the beginning of the war Price had determined to found a laboratory for testing professional 'psychics'. This resolve was reinforced during the course of the war by the sight of people attempting to peddle seances to the bereaved, and to the relatives and friends meeting trains carrying soldiers returning home on leave at Victoria station; the soldiers and their relatives were also offered all manner of amulets, talismans and 'letters of immunity' against death. It was no doubt his lasting disgust at this exploitation of human misery and anxiety that prompted him, in the 1930s, to draft with a barrister friend a 'Psychic Practitioners (Regulation) Bill'. This aimed to repeal the Witchcraft Act of 1735, amend the Vagrancy Act of 1824, under which mediums and fortune tellers were liable to prosecution, and examine, register and control professional psychics in such a way as to make fraud impossible. This, a Private Member's Bill, was dropped at the outbreak of the Second World War.

Photographic exposure

After 1919, Price continued his project of founding his national laboratory, and in 1920 he joined the Society for Psychical Research. Here he co-operated from time to time in a number of investigations with various distinguished members, among them Mrs K.M. Goldney and Dr E.J. Dingwall, an experienced – and relentless – research officer. His exposure of the 'spirit photographer' William Hope, whom he caught substituting a prepared photographic plate for the marked one he had given him, appeared in the society's *Journal* in 1922, and caused considerable controversy.

In 1923, according to his own account, he met on a train a quiet, shy, young woman later known as Stella C.; she asked if she might borrow the copy of *Light* that he had been reading, as she had had odd experiences of her own, and would like to know more about them. She turned out to be a gifted psychic, and it looks as if his subsequent work with her was what made Price take an increasing interest in establishing fact, rather than concentrate on exposing fraud. Like others who collaborated with him in this case, he became certain that the phenomena she produced were genuinely paranormal, including the curious unexplained sensations of cold reported independently at seances by Sir Julian Huxley and by Dr E.B. Strauss of St Bartholomew's Hospital.

As a result of Price's report on Stella C., he was appointed in 1925 London-based Foreign Research Officer to the American

Society for Psychical Research, and went on working for it until 1931 when, as the result of an upheaval over the integrity of a famous medium, who used the pseudonym of 'Margery', the society was temporarily split and the post abolished. 'Margery' was later found to have passed off as 'spirit fingerprints' those of her living dentist. During his tenure of the post, however, Price had used his opportunities to the full: he had travelled extensively, making contact with psychical researchers in Austria, France, Germany, Poland and elsewhere, observing their methods and discussing their results.

His own National Laboratory of Psychical Research, which he had set up in a small way in 1923, flourished, and by 1926 boasted a lively council that included distinguished foreign members, and a large laboratory with advanced scientific equipment – including

Above: some books from Harry Price's library, devoted to conjuring, Spiritualist writings and psychical research. Price gave his entire library to the University of London in 1936 on permanent loan. He never succeeded, however, in his aim to 'found, equip and endow a Department of Psychical Research' at the university

Below: 'Margery', a physical medium whom Harry Price exposed as a fraud, 'materialises' ectoplasm at a seance

apparatus for producing x-rays, infra-red light, flashlight cameras, thermographs, dictaphones, microphones, and so on. There was also an electrical chair for use in 'dark' seances, a device that automatically recorded periods when a medium was not sitting on it and could therefore be engaged in producing fraudulent phenomena.

The laboratory moved more than once. In 1930 its lease at the premises of the London Spiritualist Alliance ended and, after the Society for Psychical Research had refused to concern itself with the venture, Price took over new premises. Among the many alleged psychics investigated here was the 17-stone (110-kilogram) 'materialising medium' Helen Duncan, who produced spirit forms revealed by flashlight photographs to consist largely of cheesecloth; the weave, the selvedge and various tears and dirt marks were plain to see. Rubber gloves and a safety pin were also found; the rubber gloves presumably became the 'hands' of the materialised spirits, while the safety pin held their floating 'robes' together. Helen Duncan was thoroughly searched before she put on her one-piece black sateen seance garment, and retired to the equally thoroughly inspected cabinet in which she produced her marvels. The observers, of whom two were medical men, finally concluded that she swallowed and regurgitated the 'phantoms' – possibly, they speculated, from a secondary stomach. Price recorded that on being asked one night to agree to an examination by x-ray, the large lady rushed off, opened the front door and fled screaming down the street, hotly pursued by three professors, two doctors, and various other sitters.

In the public eye

Price's inability to refuse any challenge, however ridiculous, often led him into absurd situations. On one occasion, in 1932, he set off for the Harz mountains with Professor Joad to take part – in connection with the Goethe Centenary celebrations – in a folklore ritual in which a white billy-goat, after magical ceremonies, was supposed to turn into a handsome young man. He also could not resist the claims on his attention of Gef the 'talking mongoose', alleged to haunt an isolated farmhouse in the Isle of Man, off the coast of England. This 'beast' sang, screamed, threw things about, read the papers, laughed, and sent investigators a tuft of hair (identical with that of the family collie) and some remarkable paw prints in plasticine; but on the morning on which Price was due to visit the farm, the creature deserted it, and did not return until the researcher had departed. Nevertheless, Price was aware of the publicity value of the affair and conducted a thorough investigation into a case that most psychical researchers dismissed out of hand.

The physical medium Helen Duncan 'materialises' 'Peggy' in a seance conducted in her own home (left). The photograph clearly shows 'Peggy' to be a creature of papier-mâché and cheesecloth. Helen Duncan was investigated by Harry Price at his National Laboratory of Psychical Research in London (below); Price and his team concluded that she produced her effects by swallowing and regurgitating the materials

Below: Harry Price and Professor Joad spend a night in an allegedly haunted 16th-century bed in Chiswick, London, in 1932. Price's sense of adventure made him unable to turn down a proposition, however absurd

The price of fame

Many scientists refuse to take the work of psychical researcher Harry Price seriously, pointing to its disregard for scientific rigour and Price's own unashamed delight in publicity.

HARRY PRICE'S TEMPERAMENT did not endear him to his fellow psychical researchers; many were alienated by his flamboyance, by his self-assertiveness, and by his tendency to claim all the credit for work undertaken jointly with others – and sometimes for achievements in which he had played no part at all. This kind of behaviour might have been discounted as merely an odd quirk of Price's character – albeit an irritating one – but for an extraordinary episode that took place in 1932 to 1933.

In the 1920s Price had investigated at Munich with Baron von Schrenck-Nötzing – known to some of his British contemporaries as Baron Shrink-at-nothing – the exploits of a young Austrian psychic by the name of Willy Schneider and became increasingly convinced that some of what went on was genuinely paranormal. Later, when Willy's talents were fading – as so often happens when psychics reach maturity – Price paid several visits to the Schneider family at Braunau-am-Inn, where Willy's younger brother Rudi was apparently developing even more startling powers as a physical medium, and arranged that Rudi should come to London for tests in his laboratory. He conducted three investigations in which Lord Charles Hope, a leading member of the Society for Psychical Research, the physicist Lord John Rayleigh, and others observed the inexplicable movement of objects, some quite heavy, heard violent rappings, and apparently saw the materialised forms of 'pseudopods' resembling hands, limbs or purposeful eels in action. The last of the series of investigations took place between February and May 1932. That April, Price discovered that Lord Charles had invited Rudi to undergo yet another investigation, totally independent of its predecessors – and had not invited Price himself. It is easy to understand his anger – after all, he had done much of the preliminary work, had organised Rudi's visits to this country, and probably felt the latter was *his* discovery – but not the form it took. He waited until the new venture had been carried out and the Hope-Rayleigh report was due to appear; and then issued in the *Bulletin* of his National Laboratory for Psychical Research – and splashed in the press – an allegation that *he* had found Rudi cheating,

backing it up with some rather ambiguous flashlight photographs. This action may have been balm to his wounded pride, but was slow poison to his scientific reputation.

There has been much argument – particularly as, to this day, Rudi Schneider has not been proved to have been a fraud – as to whether Price deliberately faked the photographs, and about the fact that they are in any case open to more than one interpretation. Whatever the conclusions, it remains true that, during the many months that went by between the end of his experiments and the publication of his vengeful 'disclosure', Price had allowed various people, friends and colleagues among them, to believe in Rudi's hitherto undoubted good faith, and go ahead devoting time, energy, thought and money on the project without so much as warning them to take extra precautions.

It was this that nourished the suspicion

Below: Harry Price conducts an experiment with the young Austrian physical medium Rudi Schneider. Together with his colleague Baron von Schrenck-Nötzing (right) – known to some of his British contemporaries as Baron Shrink-at-nothing – Price, during the 1920s, conducted a series of investigations into the alleged powers of Rudi and his older brother Willy

work had been authorised by the Research Advisory Committee of the SPR, which also made a grant in aid of the expenses involved; it was based on a re-examination of the relevant files, and on interviews with as many as possible of those originally involved, and repudiated many of the accusations made in *The Borley report*. (Price himself had died in 1948: the law of libel would have protected him during his life time.) Unfortunately, *An examination of the 'Borley report'* was never published in book form, and its existence is often ignored.

Price was not unconscious of the violent antagonism he aroused. He recognised with regret his unpopularity with both Spiritualists and psychical researchers, and did not conceal the fact that he thought the SPR 'stodgy'. He continued to work on his own plans. He never succeeded in his efforts to get the University of London to accept his offer, first made in 1933, and more than once renewed, 'to found, equip and endow a Department of Psychical Research' there. Though the authorities agreed that this 'was a fit subject for investigation' – itself a

Below: Rudi Schneider in the seance room used by him and by his brother Willy at their family home in Braunau-am-Inn, in 1930. After Price had completed his experiments with Rudi, he discovered that Lord Charles Hope, a leading member of the Society for Psychical Research, had invited Rudi to undergo a further, and quite independent, series of tests. Price's reaction – for reasons that remain obscure, although they did little to endear him to his colleagues – was to splash in the press an allegation that he had already found Rudi cheating

that Price was completely ruthless, that he would even use deliberate fraud to achieve his own ends. And it was perhaps this suspicion that inspired with such venom *The haunting of Borley Rectory*, usually known as *The Borley report*, published by three of his former colleagues in 1956 both in book form and as part of the *Proceedings* of the Society for Psychical Research. It surveyed his two books, *The most haunted house in England* and *The end of Borley Rectory*. These – written at a popular level, but referring serious students to documents available for further reading – chronicled his experiences, investigations and findings at Borley, Essex, England Price visited Borley at intervals, conducting thorough investigations and searching interviews with local inhabitants, and even rented the house for an entire year during which he spent much time there with a number of volunteer researchers. In the end Price, who had suspected a certain amount of hanky-panky all along, concluded that some of the occurrences were indeed paranormal.

The case for the defence

The Borley report reads like a statement of a case for the prosecution, assuming the guilt of the prisoner at the bar throughout, interpreting evey doubtful point as evidence against him, and making various suggestions and inferences later shown not to fit in with a full knowledge of the facts. One of the allegations, that Price had buried a number of bones for subsequent 'discovery', took no account of his heart condition, which would have made heavy digging impossible.

In a later issue of the *Proceedings* of the SPR, *An examination of the 'Borley report'*, by Robert J. Hastings discussed its whole argument and its separate weaknesses. Hastings's

considerable achievement – the problem of accommodation was considered insoluble. In 1934, however, Price became the honorary secretary and editor of the University of London Council for Psychical Investigation. Late in 1936 he transferred on permanent loan to that university his magnificent collection of books, now established at Senate House as the Harry Price Library. Among its thousands of serious studies, ancient and modern, of every aspect of parapsychology is a revealing – and very funny – American catalogue with contemporary illustrations, entitled *Gambols with the ghosts*, which was circulated to mediums in 1901. Among the items on offer were 'Spirit bolts and hand-cuffs', apparatus for 'Spirit table and chair lifting' and, at $50, a 'full luminous female form (with face that convinces) which . . . appears gradually, floats about the room, and disappears'.

The laboratory was handed over to the university some months later; the equipment was never again used for research into the paranormal. The library was further enriched with a number of manuscripts, slides, photographic negatives and films. Among the latter were some dealing with the very interesting firewalking experiments Price carried out, one in 1935 with Kuda Bux, and three – the last of them televised – in 1937, with Ahmed Hussein and some volunteers. On each occasion the heat of the trench of glowing charcoal was recorded. The observers finally concluded that success in crossing it unburned depended on taking no more than four strides, with a quick decisive tread.

The acceptance of his library and laboratory by London University must have given Harry Price a sense of public recognition for his work. In 1938 he resuscitated

Right: Harry Price, with his secretary Lucie Kaye – the picture of a successful psychical researcher. In real life, however, Price's career did not live up to his ambition

Below: the bones of the nun allegedly found by Price in the cellar of Borley Rectory are re-interred in nearby Liston churchyard on 29 May 1945. It has been alleged that Price himself hid the bones for subsequent 'discovery'; but Price had a heart condition that meant that he would have had to enlist the help of a collaborator to perpetrate such a hoax

the Ghost Club, which had twice faded out since it was founded in the 19th century for the purpose of dining and discussion, and made it a society of much genial and relaxed conversation, good table talk, in which high seriousness and statistical argument played at most a minor part. He also spent much time in lecturing, writing – and of course in the protracted investigations at Borley.

This is a very brief and patchy survey of Harry Price's life and work. He clearly delighted in exposing fraud, and in demonstrating with glee the many ingenious ways in which it was perpetrated; but there has been no space in these chapters to discuss in detail every venture that he made, his meetings with mediums allegedly 'in touch with life on Mars', his investigations of dowsing both in the field and on maps, his chronicling of the stigmatic marks shown by a young Romanian poltergeist victim, Eleonore Zugun and his strong impression of having seen and touched the materialisation of a dead child, Rosalie, an impression with which he said he was 'not entirely satisfied'.

An extrovert, an originator of new ideas rather than an administrator, more interested in the circumstances and details of events than in establishing the principles underlying them, Price, whatever his limitations and his faults, brought home to a great many people that psychic phenomena do sometimes occur, and that this can and should be accepted without first finding a frame of reference into which they fit. In this, his attitude had a curious likeness to that of a very different character, Sir William Crookes, whose reply to attacks by various critics on some of his reports about D.D. Home's controversial work in levitation was 'I never said it was possible. I said it happened.'

Friendliness and beer

Price, like Crookes, tried whenever possible to find ordinary explanations for what looked like paranormal phenomena. He frequently succeeded in doing so, often by good management, sometimes by good luck – as when he found himself sitting in an Innsbruck beer garden with a troupe of wonder workers by whose performances he had been genuinely puzzled, having ruled out the use of codes, signals or machinery. Later their manager acknowledged that he had met the local inhabitants on whom miraculous 'tests' had been successfully carried out in various bars a day or two before, and enlisted their help by giving them complimentary tickets to the show and promising them free drinks. 'It was all done,' he said, *'mit Freundlichkeit und Bier'* – 'with friendliness and beer'. This ability to be amused at small-scale rogues probably helped Price's work as much as it damaged his reputation.

It is undoubtedly true that he longed – to an almost grotesque degree – to be famous, to

be universally known, recognised, discussed; but perhaps this longing did not always preponderate in the mixture of motives that governed him as mixed motives govern us all. His overwhelming interest was a desire to expose fraud, which later merged with a desire to record and examine what he called the 'very few grains of genuine phenomena which we so patiently extract from mountains of psychic chaff'. He notes that he would have lost interest in parapsychology 'many years ago if I had found nothing but fraud' but that the discovery of really paranormal incidents 'made it impossible for me ever to give up the quest of *how* these things happen and *why*'.

Right: Eleonore Zugun, a Romanian poltergeist victim whose skin showed raised weals, sometimes in the shapes of letters, when she believed she was being attacked by a devil that only she could see. She was thoroughly investigated by Price in the 1920s

Below: Ahmed Hussein, closely followed by Price and other members of his team, participate in a firewalking experiment at Carshalton, south London, on 9 April 1937

Sceptical enquirers

A sitter at a seance reels with shock as a spirit materialises before him. This kind of phenomenon has always been extremely rare – if, indeed, it has ever happened – and has been regarded by the Society for Psychical Research (SPR) with some caution. Over the years individual investigators from the society have denounced some mediums as frauds and consequently the SPR as a whole has gained a reputation as being anti-Spiritualist – and sceptical about many allied phenomena

The Society for Psychical Research celebrated its centenary in 1982. ROY STEMMAN **describes its sometimes chequered history and its continuing quest for some explanations for paranormal phenomena**

SPIRITUALISM HAD SWEPT across the Atlantic and settled itself comfortably in the parlours of some of the best English families by the late 1870s. The wonders of the seance room were seldom out of the headlines and appeared to be little short of miraculous. Minds could communicate with other minds. Objects could vanish and reappear. Spirits could materialise and talk with the living. And a life hereafter was guaranteed for everyone.

It was against this exciting if bewildering background, rife with fraud and self-delusion, that a group of scientists, scholars and Spiritualists got together on 5 January 1882 to form the British Society for Psychical Research (SPR).

Although the society was conceived at a meeting in the rooms of the British National Association of Spiritualists, its earliest work was more concerned with experiments in thought transference and the study of spontaneous psychic phenomena than with mediums or communicating with the dead.

Membership of the first SPR Council (the society was formally constituted on 20 February 1882) is indicative of the calibre of person it then attracted. President was

Letty Hyde. d. 1. xi. 1921. Photo taken Sept 1924.
Sitters L to R. Sir Wm Barrett. F.R.S., Miss Scatchard, S. De
Brath. Mediums. Wm Hope and Mrs Buxton. Plates specially
marked and packet taped & double-sealed by the Imperial
Plate Co. Development by S. De Brath. M. Inst. C.E.
Letty Hyde

The founder members of the SPR were dissatisfied with extreme reactions to paranormal phenomena – crass credulity on the one hand and irrational scepticism on the other – and were determined to form a society that would establish new and high standards of investigation. Among the first members were (below left) W. Stainton Moses, a clergyman who was also a medium; (left, seen here with his son) Frederic W. H. Myers, a classical scholar from Cambridge; (above left, seated on the left) Sir William Barrett, a professor of physics who considered this photograph absolute proof of the genuineness of some psychic photographs; (above) Frank Podmore, an author who later became an outspoken sceptic, and (above right) G. W. Balfour, who was president of the SPR from 1906 to 1907

Henry Sidgwick, an outstanding Cambridge professor of classics with a well-deserved reputation as a critic and sceptic.

Among the other 18 council members were Sir William Barrett, professor of physics at the Royal College of Science in Dublin (who was responsible for calling the meeting that established the SPR); Frederic W.H. Myers, an eminent classical scholar who had studied under Sidgwick at Cambridge; Edmund Gurney, also a classical scholar; W. Stainton Moses, a clergyman turned schoolmaster who was a celebrated medium; and Frank Podmore, author and one-time Spiritualist – who was to become an outspoken sceptic.

Shades of the Ghost Society

Many of the SPR's early supporters had been actively engaged in exploring psychic subjects for some time before its creation, through their connection with the Ghost Society at Cambridge – Myers and Gurney were members, as were many other early leaders of the SPR.

They all shared an intense interest in the deeper questions of life at a time when materialism seemed destined to erode religious beliefs. Most of them, as a result of personal experiences, were predisposed towards a belief in the existence of psychic phenomena, but their critical approach, particularly to mediums, soon resulted in many leading Spiritualists leaving the SPR.

The SPR has retained to this day an image of a learned, scientific and rather 'stuffy' body, which refuses to believe virtually every claim of paranormality. In fact, the society holds no corporate opinion, but its members, officers and committees most certainly do –

and some, over the years, have publicly declared their belief in the genuineness of a variety of psychical phenomena.

Apart from collecting material for a major survey, which was later published as *Phantasms of the living* (see box), the SPR also tackled another side of psychical research: the claims by some individuals to be able to produce physical phenomena, usually under conditions that made verification difficult.

When SPR members had sittings with William Eglinton, a contemporary medium, during which he was said to produce spirit writings on slates, several believed the results to be paranormal. Mrs Sidgwick and Dr Richard Hodgson, a young Australian researcher, were unconvinced, however, and said so in the SPR's *Journal*, which led to a heated controversy and some resignations.

Where physical phenomena were concerned, Hodgson was very sceptical and his refusal to accept at face value a favourable report by Sir Oliver Lodge on his experiences with an Italian medium, Eusapia Palladino, led to an invitation to her to visit England to be studied by the SPR.

Lodge, together with F.W.H. Myers, had attended seances conducted by Palladino in 1894 at the home of Professor Charles Richet in France and both were satisfied she was genuine. They persuaded Professor Sidgwick and his wife to witness some of the seances and they were also impressed. But when their report was published in the SPR *Journal*, Hodgson was highly critical.

In an attempt to settle the matter, the SPR arranged for Palladino to give a series of seances at Cambridge, England, starting on 31 July 1895. Palladino obliged by cheating. At a later seance, however, Myers found her genuine. The matter was never resolved.

While the SPR's researchers were seeking for the truth about psychic phenomena in the dark seance rooms of Cambridge and Naples,

Above: Eleanor Sidgwick, one of the SPR's founders

Below: a Victorian catalogue advertising 'self playing guitars' and 'sealed letter reading' – for a fee

the sceptical Dr Richard Hodgson was in the U.S. studying a remarkable 'mental' medium, Mrs Leonore Piper, who appeared to communicate with the dead.

The American Society for Psychical Research (ASPR) – which was also founded on Professor William Barrett's initiative, in 1885 – had been studying Mrs Piper for several years, but when its research programme became too expensive, in 1889, it became a branch of the SPR in London, subsidised by its parent; as a result it was arranged for Mrs Piper and her daughters to winter in England to give a series of seances.

Elaborate precautions were taken to ensure that Mrs Piper could not acquire information about her hosts or their friends during her stay, and she was accompanied everywhere she went. Though the SPR committee that investigated her could not agree on the origin of her trance utterances (which purported to be from a spirit), they were unanimous in their opinion that they 'show that knowledge has been acquired by some intelligence in some supernormal fashion. . . .'

A literary puzzle

The ASPR was able to study Mrs Piper for 30 years, and she returned to England in 1906, again at the SPR's invitation, for further tests. During the early years of this century she also made an important contribution to a series of automatic writing scripts that have come to be known as the 'cross correspondences'.

Soon after the death of F.W.H. Myers in 1901, a number of mediums began receiving automatic scripts; in themselves they were meaningless, but they appeared to fit together like a literary jigsaw puzzle. The spirit author who controlled their hands claimed to be Myers.

Over a 30-year period more than 3000

The quest begins

One of the most important research projects in the SPR's early days was a study of spontaneous psychical phenomena. This resulted in the publication, in 1886, of *Phantasms of the living*, a two-volume work that ran to 1300 pages, by Gurney, Myers and Podmore. The book remains a classic in the annals of psychical research.

Many of the cases investigated in its pages concerned 'crisis apparitions' – hearing or seeing a vision of a person at a time when that person was experiencing a crisis or dying – and it led to the theory that such apparitions were created by telepathy.

Three years later, Professor Sidgwick reported that an SPR committee's investigation had produced 1200 pages of evidence supporting the reality of telepathy, and in the same year, 1889, a 'census of hallucinations' began under his guidance.

Sidgwick's wife, helped by Miss Alice Johnson, did most of the work of collating the results of a question put to 17,000 people asking if, while awake, they had experienced a sensation of seeing or being touched by a living being or inanimate object, or hearing a voice, for which there was no obvious physical cause.

Analysis of the results showed that 1684 people had, among them, experienced 1942 hallucinations, 300 of which related to visions of individuals they recognised. In 80 of these cases the person seen had died within 12 hours, before or after the hallucination. In 32 instances, the person experiencing the vision had mentioned it to a third party before news of the death was received.

scripts were produced by seven principal mediums, all of whom – with the exception of Mrs Piper – were non-professional. The work of collecting and collating the scripts from these mediums, who lived in various parts of Britain, the United States, India and Egypt, was the largest and most elaborate research project ever undertaken by the SPR.

For reasons of space and privacy, the greater part of the scripts has never been published, but the view of those most familiar with them is that they do have a single pattern running through them. Whether that pattern was imposed by the discarnate Myers, or whether a more mundane theory of psychical connections between the mediums is the answer, remains an open question.

By the early part of the 20th century, English SPR members had a medium in their midst whose abilities were very similar to those of Mrs Piper. Gladys Osborne Leonard was an actress who discovered she possessed mediumistic talents. In 1918 she placed her services at the disposal of an SPR committee, with very favourable results.

The period between the two world wars proved to be the heyday of physical phenomena, and the SPR was kept busy studying the top international mediums, including 'Eva C' (the pseudonym of the French materialisation medium Marthe Beraud) in 1920; Willi Schneider, from Austria, in 1924, and his brother Rudi in 1932, and Margery Crandon, from the U.S., in 1923 – to name only a few who gave seances in London for the society.

As well as the London studies of these mediums, SPR officers went abroad to watch them at work. Dr Eric Dingwall, the SPR's research officer in 1922, visited Munich to attend seances with Willi Schneider and was present, two years later, when the young

Gladys Osborne Leonard, an actress who became a very powerful physical medium. In 1918 – when many unscrupulous fake mediums were exploiting the despair and grief from the war – she offered herself to the SPR for investigation. On the whole, their findings were in her favour

Austrian demonstrated his powers in London for the SPR.

Although the phenomena were not impressive, Dingwall's report stated that the investigators were 'driven to the conclusion that the only reasonable hypothesis which covers the facts is that some supernormal agency produced the results'.

In 1932, Willi's brother Rudi gave 27 seances for the society in London during which infra-red equipment was used, unsuccessfully, to detect psychic manifestations. Nevertheless, some observers were impressed by the occurrence of telekinetic phenomena, such as the movement of a table.

The price of fame

The SPR did not have a monopoly as far as investigations into the paranormal were concerned. There was also Harry Price, the flamboyant independent investigator with a knack of gaining publicity, who ran the National Laboratory of Psychical Research.

Much of Price's research work is now regarded with suspicion – including his 'exposure' of Rudi Schneider – but his discovery and investigation of a young English medium, Stella Cranshaw, made an important contribution to psychical research.

SPR observers attended some of the Cranshaw seances, and she also gave two seances especially for the society, in 1923. Dr Dingwall, present at one of the sessions, testified later that he observed a curious, and apparently genuine, phenomenon:

From near the medium's foot . . . I saw an egg-shaped body begin to crawl towards the centre of the floor under the table. It was white, and where the light was reflected it appeared opal. To the end nearest the medium was attached a thin white neck like a piece of

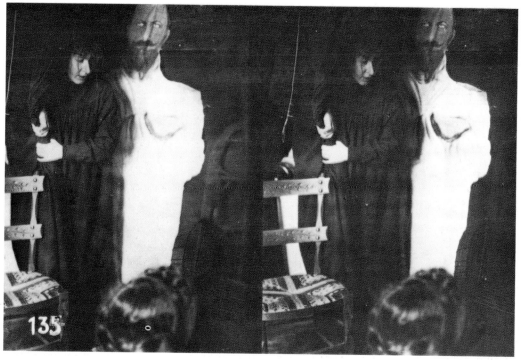

Far left and left: two stages in the alleged materialisation of the spirit 'Dorsmica', through the mediumship of 'Eva C', the French physical medium whose real name was Marthe Beraud. She was investigated by the SPR in 1920; in many ways her mediumship raised questions characteristic of psychical research as a whole. The evidence here – the materialisation – looks blatantly fake, but investigation found no proof that it was. The mystery remained unsolved

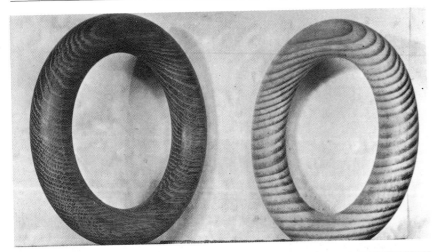

macaroni. It advanced towards the centre and then rapidly withdrew to the shadow. . . .

Those involved in psychical research at that time were unaware that they were witnessing the end of an era: for whatever reasons, physical phenomena have now virtually disappeared, at least on the scale experienced in the 1930s and 1940s.

The trend towards ESP research, so much a concern of the SPR's founders, began in the 1940s, influenced by the pioneering work of Dr J.B. Rhine in the United States. New and more sophisticated techniques were now available to study telepathy, clairvoyance and precognition.

Cards on the table

G.N.M. Tyrrell, an electrical engineer (the SPR president from 1945 to 1946), devised a machine for testing ESP using lights in boxes and giving an automatic trace recording of the results. His adopted daughter was the subject and she produced impressive results.

Next came a series of experiments, conducted between 1941 and 1943 by Dr S.G. Soal and Mrs K.M. Goldney with Basil Shackleton. These straightforward telepathy tests, using a pack of cards with five different designs, appeared to show a remarkable 'displacement' effect – something that had been reported by other researchers – indicating that Shackleton was using clairvoyance to detect a card before it was selected by random number tables.

The Soal-Goldney results were regarded as one of the most impressive contributions to ESP research for years, but a reassessment has thrown considerable doubt on the accuracy of the experiments, suggesting that Soal 'fudged' the results to make them appear impressive.

Since the 1960s, even greater sophistication has been brought to bear on the research work carried out under the SPR's auspices or reported in its *Journal*. Radioactive degeneration has been used to introduce randomness in precognition tests, Dr John Beloff of Edinburgh University (SPR president from 1974 to 1976) pioneering such

When medium Margery Crandon demonstrated that solid wooden rings (top) could interlock (above), Sir Oliver Lodge believed this was a 'blow for materialist scientists'. The rings, however, separated again. Dr John Beloff (centre) says that anomalous phenomena such as permanently linked rings would be the ideal centrepiece of a museum of the paranormal

research in Britain in 1961. Altered states of consciousness have been explored in the search for psychic powers, and electronics have come to the aid of PK researchers.

The paranormal seems to have been wrested from the seance room and placed firmly in the laboratory where, as far as the layman is concerned, it is likely to be buried beneath a welter of statistics, theories and equations – which make it seem very remote from the vivid spontaneous phenomena that many people experience. Psychical research and its related field work is being replaced with a cold and clinical parapsychology.

But perhaps that is not a bad thing, if it succeeds in capturing elusive paranormal powers and making them work to order, as Julian Isaacs is seeking to do with his British minilab programme (see page 22). Then perhaps science will take seriously the suggestion of Sir Alister Hardy (SPR president from 1965 to 1969), in his presidential address to the zoological section of the British Association for the Advancement of Science in 1949. He argued that telepathy could have great relevance to biological studies, and he enlarged on that theory later by suggesting that if telepathy is accepted 'then we must expect something akin to it . . . to mould the patterns of behaviour among members of all species.' And in 1981 a new SPR member, Dr Rupert Sheldrake, proposed a controversial and dramatic new theory of evolution that could, if proved to have a factual basis, provide the 'something akin' to telepathy in

other species that Sir Alister Hardy was hoping for.

But the SPR holds no 'official' opinions. Its members are free to believe or disbelieve what they like. Its attitude was summed up by Sir Oliver Lodge (SPR president from 1901 to 1903) and his words still epitomise the SPR's uncompromising approach: '. . . it is better to hesitate too long over a truth than to welcome an error, for a false gleam may lead us far astray unless it is soon detected.'

The impossible dream?

The Society for Psychical Research has always tried to apply the strictest scientific methods to the investigation of paranormal phenomena. But, asks BRIAN INGLIS, is this a mistaken attempt to ingratiate the society with the scientific establishment?

WHEN THE SOCIETY for Psychical Research (SPR) was launched in 1882 its founders – in particular, those who were in the academic world – were confronted by two main problems. The first, as Frederic Myers was later to recall, was to impress scientists with the reality of what he called 'supernormal' phenomena (in order to avoid the more vague other-wordly implications of 'super-natural'). The unexplained phenomena the society intended to study were, Myers was sure, *natural*: even if they were not normal. This meant that they must be discovered and investigated 'by no analysis of tradition, and by no manipulation of metaphysics, but simply by experiment and observation'. The second problem was to find how to experiment, and how to observe, applying 'precisely the same methods of deliberate, dispassionate, exact inquiry which have built up our actual knowledge of the world which we can touch and see' – but applying them to phenomena that did not behave in ways familiar in the world we can touch and see.

Since 1882 scientific methodology has been employed by psychical researchers and it has demonstrated the existence of ESP, PK and other psychic, or 'psi', phenomena. And even the most rock-ribbed sceptics – if they deigned to study the original reports – would feel obliged to take the phenomena more seriously than they do. But few sceptics are inclined to 'waste' their time going back to source.

But here comes the irony. As opinion polls have shown with impressive consistency, the public in Britain and in the USA now accepts the reality of what are currently known as *paranormal* phenomena. It accepts some phenomena more readily than others, admittedly; but it overwhelmingly accepts that there are more things in heaven and earth than common scientific teaching – or even common sense – allows for. Yet, even so, the work of psychical researchers is given little credit. The common image of the SPR is of a bunch of well-intentioned lunatics.

Since the late 1970s the society has been split by a feud that arose out of divided opinions as to whether it should stay in its academic ivory tower, or reach out for more popular support and recognition. This has led to the 'popular' faction splitting off to

Above: a scientific ESP experiment, of the sort popularised by J.B. Rhine in the United States. Card guessing, however, has proved to be unpopular with those who are best at it – the psychics – for the simple reason that it is boring. This is one of the major problems of psychical research – either the phenomena are spontaneous and unrepeatable or they soon peter out in the clinical atmosphere of the laboratory. Should psychical researchers bravely abandon all attempts to use established scientific methods or should they hold out for the elusive 'proof' that may or may not materialise?

form their own organisation – the Association for the Scientific Study of Anomalous Phenomena (ASSAP), which was inaugurated in 1981. There can consequently be no doubt that the SPR remains committed, at least for the foreseeable future, to adhere to Myers's formula of 'deliberate, dispassionate, exact inquiry', along traditional academic lines.

Hitting out blindly

This leaves the society with three problems, the first being – as it has been from its foundation – the continuing existence of academic scepticism about the paranormal; based not on reasonable doubts about the evidence, but upon what can only be described as an unreasoning fear of its implications, which overturn so much of what has been scientific gospel for two centuries. And this has led otherwise rational people to behave in highly unscientific, and sometimes manifestly dishonest, ways. Anybody who thinks that scientists and academics in general have been taking a detached, dispassionate view of psychical research should read the survey by sociologists Harry Collins and Tom Pinch of Bath University, which appeared in *On the margins of science*, edited by Roy Wallis and published in 1978 by the University of Keele.

Collins and Pinch were not concerned with the argument about whether or not paranormal phenomena exist. On that issue, they insisted, they were deliberately neutral. What they were investigating was 'the processes involved in the attempt to establish the existence of a certain class of phenomena'; and this led them to examine the ways that sceptics have used to discredit that attempt, ranging from flat refusal to accept the evidence on a priori grounds, to insinuations of fraud and the 'smearing' of researchers' reputations – often in the crudest and most childish ways.

One result of this is that many psychical researchers have found it extremely difficult to get their work published, except in the society's own *Journal*. The only material that has been considered acceptable for publication elsewhere is accounts that denigrate psychical research.

Psychical researchers have also had to contend with the Committee for the Scientific Investigation of Claims of the Paranormal (CSICOP), set up in the United States, but with an active branch in Britain, which in practice has been concerned only to discredit them. However, CSICOP's reputation

received a devastating blow from one of its founder members in 1980 when it was disclosed that one of CSICOP's trials confirmed, rather than overturned, the positive findings of the French researcher Michel Gauquelin about the traditional 'Mars effect' of astrology. The results, against the member's advice, had been suppressed. This is a disclosure from which CSICOP will surely find it hard to recover.

The psychical researchers' second major problem remains as it was in 1882: how to apply scientific rules in researching phenomena that do not obey scientific rules – or, indeed, any rules known to Man.

In *My philosophy*, written when he was in his eighties – but still evidently in full possession of his faculties – Sir Oliver Lodge warned that the kind of controls that orthodox science has demanded in psychical research – for example, as exemplified in the

Top: the advanced version of the table designed by psychical researcher Colin Brookes-Smith to detect any unconscious muscular activity on the part of sitters at table-tilting sessions. It is seen here with the top removed

Above: the electronic device used by Dr John Beloff of Edinburgh University to test for ESP. The machine randomly lights one of five hidden lamps; the subject then switches in his guess. An alternative experiment involves the subject trying to predict which lamp the machine will select

extraordinary measures taken to restrain mediums physically in order to prevent fraud – were counter-productive. This was partly because when the aim of the test was to see whether the medium could exert a psychokinetic force, objects would not necessarily move within the test area – but if they did move outside it, critics would jump to the conclusion that the necessary precautions had been neglected.

In any case, Lodge feared sceptics would never accept the evidence 'even if every member of the company had been searched and handcuffed with all their utterances recorded on a gramophone, and all their movements on a revolving drum'. Half a century later, events have confirmed that he was justified in his pessimism.

Herein lies the main danger to the SPR, in its role as a strictly scientific body. Its members' energies are likely to be concentrated on research of a kind that is designed to make a scientific breakthrough. But this, as one of the most respected members of the Parapsychological Association – the international body set up in 1957 – warned in 1980 in a letter he sent out to a number of its members, is going to be dangerous, because it is likely to lead to more attempts to collaborate with the establishment; and this, in turn, will encourage the adoption of scientific assumptions and methods that are not merely irrelevant in parapsychology, but are actually destructive.

This leads to the SPR's third major problem. As a primarily academic body, it is singularly ill-fitted to investigate spontaneous events. A century ago university professors and lecturers had the leisure to pursue such investigations, if they so wished;

but few of them have the time to do so today.

And the SPR does not provide any training courses; those few members who are experienced in dealing with, for example, poltergeist cases have no time to investigate new ones, let alone train new investigators. Attempts are now being made to remedy this deficiency; but it may well be that members of ASSAP will be more willing – and better able – to take on such work.

Poltergeist power

Poltergeists also show up another weakness of the attempt to pursue psi along currently accepted scientific lines: they refuse to play the game according to the scientific rules. When Guy Lyon Playfair and Maurice Grosse investigated the Enfield poltergeist (see box), they found – as many a psychical researcher has done before – that they were apparently dealing with a practical joker, who delighted in sabotaging their monitoring equipment; the damage was often done in ingenious ways, as if the poltergeist were determined to demonstrate that it could use PK to cause faults in instruments in ways that could not conceivably be attributed to chance breakdowns.

Playfair has said that the only diabolical thing about his Enfield experience was the train service to and from London; but there are times when psychical researchers can be forgiven for thinking that some demon is deliberately working against them, to spoil their case – the 'ink fish effect', as writer Arthur Koestler has described it, referring to the way that an octopus eludes predators at the last moment by exuding an inky cloud.

Attempts have also been made to fulfil the demands of scientific protocol by imposing ever stricter controls, only to be haunted by another spectre – the 'psi experimenter effect' in which the 'psi' itself eludes controls, confusing the experimental results. Perhaps Sir Oliver Lodge was right to warn fellow members of the SPR that uncontrolled trials must not be despised, because it may be that, under less than strict conditions, 'phenomena occur of such vigour, and of so simple and striking a character, that they overcome suspicion, and constitute their own demonstration'. But this sort of research needs endless patience, and is labour-intensive. This author, for one, cannot see the SPR – at least in its present condition – being willing and able to cope with such a workload. Mutual suspicion and personality clashes will, no doubt, make co-operation between the SPR and ASSAP difficult for a time; but they must surely attempt to reconcile some of their differences if the quest to understand the elusive nature of psi is to be effectively pursued.

None so blind...

The investigation of the Enfield poltergeist by author Guy Lyon Playfair and businessman Maurice Grosse – both members of the SPR – has given rise to much bitterness among members. To many, the lengthy investigation, which is described in detail in Guy Lyon Playfair's *This house is haunted* (1980), was both ethical and scrupulously fair. To others, especially some members of the society's council, it seemed plain that the children involved were playing tricks. In fact, both Playfair and Grosse have admitted in print that the children had been discovered to be cheating on occasion, but still maintain that what they were doing was merely *imitating* the real and terrifying phenomena they experienced almost daily for many months. These included the apparently mysterious burning of a jumper (left) and the denting of a teapot that, it was claimed, had been hurled across the room by an invisible agency (above left).

Some of the critics never even visited the disturbed house, provoking Maurice Grosse to remark in a letter to the society's *Journal*: 'I am led to wonder if some members of this Society are prepared to admit the existence of the phenomena the Society was formed to study.'

The way ahead

The Society for Psychical Research has weathered 100 years of controversy and even confusion. A.J. ELLISON, the society's president in its centenary year, assesses its continuing problems – and its positive contributions

THE FOUNDERS of the Society for Psychical Research (SPR) set out in 1882 with high hopes that the work of the society, firmly based on the well-established methods of science, would lead to answers to some of the most basic, important and perennial questions of humanity. Does the human personality survive bodily death? Are human beings in touch with each other in ways independent of the bodily senses? And so on.

What is the situation today? People often ask, in relation to the work of the SPR, 'Well, after 100 years, what do you really know?' The answer is, we know a great deal.

Scientific research is a process of asking questions of nature. In some areas we have

Above: the head office of the Society for Psychical Research (SPR) at 1 Adam and Eve Mews, off Kensington High Street in west London. The building houses an impressive library (right), which stores one of the world's most comprehensive collections of books on telepathy, mediumship, life after death, hypnosis, dreams, out-of-the-body experiences, poltergeists, apparitions and allied phenomena

discovered that we may have been asking nature the wrong questions, or inappropriate questions. Distinguished researching members of the SPR have usually been very cautious in their replies to questions asking for conclusions. And they have not been at all ready to accept facile answers to questions that may be much more complex than the questioner realises. The result of this has been that the SPR has acquired a reputation for inordinate scepticism, an inability to accept anything at face value. But there was always good reason for this attitude even though it was often misunderstood. This point can be well-illustrated with examples.

Who goes there?

'Do you believe in ghosts?' Usually when this question is asked the questioner has in his mind the traditional idea of a ghost: a 'dead' person wandering around the physical world in some sort of ethereal next-world body. This is the popular idea of ghosts – but the SPR's researchers have discovered that seeing a 'ghost' is almost always *an hallucinatory experience*. Only if the question were re-worded as 'Do you believe that people sometimes experience apparitions?' would modern psychical researchers answer 'Yes'. It would, however, be an emphatic affirmative for there is plenty of good evidence that people do see such apparitions.

Two early surveys carried out by SPR members showed that about 10 per cent of the people who replied did believe in the existence of apparations. Later surveys gave somewhat similar responses., The difficult part is the explanation. What causes people occasionally to have an experience like that? Probably there are different causes for the

Right: some lines of automatic script, allegedly from a dead SPR member, Dr Richard Hodgson, through the mediumship of Mrs Piper. Although the SPR is reputed to be somewhat sceptical about claims of communication from the dead, arguably some of the best evidence for an afterlife is to be found in its 'cross-correspondences'

Below: *The psychic dance*, a cartoon by Heath Robinson. The society's own social functions, however, are considerably more conventional

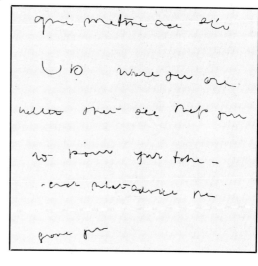

different types of apparition – 'haunting', 'telepathic', 'crisis' and 'experimental'. But, as psychical researchers have found out, apparitions are not very often much to do with 'dead' people.

Another frequent cause of misunderstanding between the SPR and the public – and in particular Spiritualists – concerns mediumistic evidence relating to survival after death. Often the SPR has been accused of being frankly biased against mediums and sceptical about any sort of afterlife. But this view is based on the SPR investigators' meticulous and objective sifting of the evidence – and the discovery that in many alleged communications other factors, such as telepathy among the living, play a major role. For example, if a medium says that she 'sees' – through her clairvoyance – a 'discarnate communicator', and if she then 'hears' –

through her clairaudience – information such as might be passed on by such an ostensible communicator, and if the sitter recognises this information, it is usually suggested that this is proof of the presence of the surviving communicator (a 'spirit'). If the psychical researcher suggests caution before drawing such a conclusion, then this, it is suggested, is more evidence of inordinate and unreasonable scepticism. But that is not true. It is quite possible, and is probably frequently the case, to have apparently satisfactory seances with no one from the 'next world' taking part at all.

Dr S.G. Soal appeared to be receiving excellent evidence from his deceased brother Frank via the control personality – the 'spirit guide' – of the trance medium Mrs Blanche Cooper. Memories, shared and long forgotten, were recalled to his mind by the 'communicating' Frank. However, Dr Soal went away and devised a completely fictitious character whom he called James Ferguson, imagining all sorts of incidents in the life of this character. When James Ferguson was very clear in his mind Dr Soal made another appointment with Mrs Cooper. The control

personality welcomed Soal and said that he had another communicator with him. The new communicator gave all sorts of facts to prove that he really had lived on earth. He was, he said, James Ferguson – but the only life he had ever lived had been in Dr Soal's imagination.

The Irish poet W.B. Yeats was once having a sitting with the well-known automatic writing medium Geraldine Cummins. He got a story 'from the other side' that did not seem of any particular interest and Geraldine Cummins asked him if she should continue. 'Yes,' he said, 'that is the plot of my new book.' Philip, the imaginary 'ghost' created in Toronto, was also able to 'communicate' by table rapping – to produce both information and physical phenomena – but only provided most of the sitters continued to 'believe' in his existence.

Truth and consequences

Yet the evidence for survival is very good, and is to be found in the voluminous papers of F. Myers and others, known as the cross correspondences, in the SPR archives. An authentic discarnate communicator certainly cannot always be ruled out. Probably it is right to consider a good sitting with a medium to consist of a mixed bag of telepathy with the sitter, the general ESP of the medium, the medium's own conscious and unconscious guesses, feedback from the sitter to the medium, and perhaps some signs of a genuine communicator somewhere in the background. Considerable experience is needed to sort out the components of an average sitting. In almost all cases, the explanation is not nearly as simple as it seems and frequently the researcher seems confronted by confusion. It is clear why strictly controlled laboratory tests were devised to try to establish exactly what is going on.

A member of the SPR cannot leave a consideration of the difficulties inherent in mediumship without paying a tribute to the Spiritualist movement in general, and mediums in particular. When scientific tests are needed to try to solve some of these deep

Just some of the SPR's archives, which contain files on many of the most famous cases of psychical research – as well as thousands of notes on little-known examples of extraordinary phenomena

conventional scientists that the editor of *Nature* denounced it as a 'book for burning'. Dr Sheldrake's revolutionary hypothesis of formative causation proposes that morphogenetic fields are responsible for evolution, learning – and *memory* – in living things. If the hypothesis proves to have a basis in fact then a great many cherished beliefs of established science will be demolished.

But despite these glittering promises, the SPR occasionally has difficulties, especially, and usually, related to the rigorous maintenance of those scientific standards of accuracy, objectivity and balance, which are now traditionally associated with it. In this approach it is unique among psychical research groups in Britain and most of the members feel that these standards must never be lowered merely in order to court popularity.

So perhaps there has never been a more auspicious time to join in the search for answers to some of humanity's deepest questions. The SPR is in good shape and good heart for its next century.

psychological mysteries, mediums have always been ready to volunteer.

But although the questions raised by mediumistic communications remain largely unanswered, many modern researchers feel that other aspects of the paranormal are more likely to yield conclusive answers. Among the younger generation of professional parapsychologists telepathy and psychokinesis (PK) are the main areas of study.

Dr Carl Sargent at Cambridge University has convincingly shown that even 'non-psychic' people can become receptive to telepathy when outside stimuli are blocked out by sensory deprivation in what is known as the Ganzfeld state. And he has confirmed the work of other researchers that shows that telepathic awareness can be *learned*.

Brave new thinkers

At the University of Aston in Birmingham Julian Isaacs is maintaining high academic standards in his search for metal benders. He has discovered that psi is much more common in everyday life than has previously been believed. And his British minilab programme if successful, will provide irrefutable proof of PK.

There are other highly respected scientists from many disciplines whose work is throwing the mechanistic school of thought into confusion – and shedding light on many of the deeper questions of life. One of the most eminent of these is Professor John Hasted, a renowned physicist of Birkbeck College, London, whose work, both in the theory and practice of paranormal metal bending, has done much to edge psychical research into academic respectability.

And quite outstanding among the brave new thinkers is Dr Rupert Sheldrake, a young plant physiologist whose book *A new science of life* (1981) caused such a stir among

Two of the SPR's members who look set to make major contributions to psychical research – as well as to more orthodox fields of science – are Julian Isaacs (left), who has devised 'fool-proof' methods of detecting PK, and Dr Rupert Sheldrake (below), who proposes that morphogenetic fields are responsible for evolution – and that memories are stored in them

In the eye of the beholder

Can the scientist remain detached from the phenomena he studies? Or is he so bound up with them that he actually creates the effects that he observes? A. J. ELLISON explores an idea that challenges scientific orthodoxy

A DISTURBING IDEA has gained currency in certain scientific circles in recent years. It is an idea that conflicts completely with the basis on which most scientists conduct their experiments, the basis of 'naïve realism'. Most scientists, most of the time, assume that the physical world is 'out there', quite independent of themselves (though the scientist's own body, with its sense organs, is clearly a part of that world). Science is considered to be, firstly, a process of describing that physical world, and then of devising hypotheses as to how things work. If the hypotheses are good ones, they stand up under test, and assume the status of established theory. For example, the movements of the planets and other celestial bodies could be predicted with considerable accuracy by Newton's theory of gravitation which, after two centuries of successes, came to be regarded as unshakeable knowledge. When hypotheses do not stand up under test they are changed, or scrapped and replaced by better ones. Thus increasingly precise measurement showed Newton's gravitational theory to be inaccurate and it was replaced by Einstein's fundamentally different general theory of relativity of 1915, which now holds the field.

An experiment in psychokinesis (PK) under way in the parapsychological laboratory directed by J.B. Rhine, who is making notes. The results that he obtained in dice-rolling experiments convinced him that subjects could mentally control the numbers that turned up on the dice. If this can happen in a deliberately contrived PK experiment, could it also happen, unknown to the experimenters, in conventional research?

Most scientists would probably be willing to accept that, when constructing their theories, they were actually building mental 'models' representing experience. But they would probably react violently against the suggestion that the realist's view is not the whole truth about science. And if it were suggested that perhaps their mental activity could affect the results of an experiment they would probably be completely incredulous and point out that a most important step in the establishment of a scientific theory is that the relevant experiments should be repeatable by other experimenters in other laboratories, to provide the assurance that the result obtained was not the product of chance, error or self-deception.

The attitude of modern nuclear physicists is perhaps a little different. In the models they have devised to explain the behaviour of elementary particles some very strange things happen. Time runs backwards, and particles may disappear at one place and reappear in another without crossing the space between. Nuclear physicists on the whole do not worry too much about the physical interpretation of their equations, believing that, provided they lead to correct predictions of the outcome of experiments, their interpretation does not matter. Their mental models cannot be visualised – they are abstract and mathematical. The bizarre nature of their theories seems to predispose physicists to be more open-minded than other scientists in paranormal questions.

The theories themselves also seem to give room for paranormal happenings. It is an old

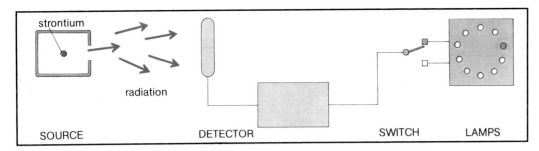

Left: the chain of events that takes place in Helmut Schmidt's PK experiments with a radioactive source. Radioactivity from strontium 90 triggers a detector, which controls a rapidly oscillating switch. The equipment is adjusted so that there is a 50 per cent chance of the switch being in either of its two positions. Lamps are lit up in a clockwise or an anticlockwise direction according to the position of the switch. Some subjects succeed in influencing the lamps to light in a particular direction. But in doing this, are they influencing the strontium, the detector, or some other part of the intricate circuitry?

Right: Helmut Schmidt at work with a random number generating device

idea that, just as everything we can learn about or become aware of in the Universe influences us, directly or indirectly – otherwise we could not gain knowledge about it – so we influence everything else in the Universe, to some degree at least. In quantum mechanics this takes on a new twist. Some of the most eminent of physicists have claimed that, when a nuclear particle is observed by a scientist – or, perhaps, when a measurement is made on it by an automatic instrument – the observation directly affects the particle: if, for example, its position is measured, the particle acquires a definite position at that moment – having previously been in an indefinite, 'spread-out' state. On this view scientists intervene very directly in the phenomena they study – they create them as much as observe them.

Searching for PK

Such an interpretation of the process of measurement in quantum physics is not accepted by all scientists – the problems surrounding the question are profound and intricate. But many psychical researchers have been encouraged to look for the effects of influences of the mind on physical processes – psychokinesis, or PK – on the micro-level. One of these is Helmut Schmidt, who built a test machine using radioactive decay. The radioactive emissions from a sample of strontium 90 controlled a number of lamps arranged in a circle. When a Geiger counter recorded the arrival of radiation from the strontium, the equipment switched off the lamp that was illuminated at that moment, and switched on a neighbouring lamp. A rapidly oscillating switch determined whether the neighbouring lamp in the clockwise or in the counterclockwise direction was lit. Schmidt's subjects were asked to try to influence the lamps to light up in a specific direction – say, clockwise – and his results indicated very strongly that they could.

Psychical researchers have noticed apparent effects of mind on matter for many years, and many other experiments have been carried out to study the phenomenon. Dr Gertrude Schmeidler found, in experiments that have been repeated many times, that subjects who had a belief in the possibility of psychic phenomena were more likely to be successful. Equally remarkable, subjects who strongly disbelieved in the very possibility of such phenomena were more likely to get results that were worse than

would be expected by chance. This too involves an interaction of an unknown type between the subject and the system that the subject is trying to observe or influence. Schmeidler called the believing subjects 'sheep' and the disbelieving ones 'goats'.

The psychical researchers have also put each other under scrutiny. Some researchers frequently get good results with their subjects: they are referred to as 'catalysts'. (The term comes from chemistry, and refers to a substance that promotes some reaction between other substances.) Other experimenters regularly fail to demonstrate PK effects, and have been described, unflatteringly, as 'inhibitors'. Usually such experimenters claim to be open-minded on the possibility of psychic phenomena occurring in their

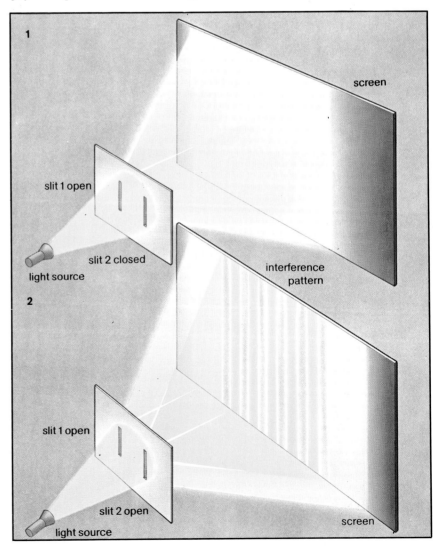

experiments: if, therefore, they are causing their own lack of success, one reason may lie in their unconscious minds.

Sceptics might suggest that the results of the 'catalysts' are actually due to fraud or incompetence. But many of these experimenters have unblemished reputations in other scientific fields: the doubters' speculations cannot be seriously entertained.

Many experiments have verified that the beliefs of subjects and experimenters are factors to be taken into account when conducting experiments in ESP and PK. The effects created by the 'Philip' group in Toronto, Canada, provide a good example of this effect. There, the deliberate use of the imagination by a group of people, none of whom claimed to have exceptional psychic abilities, created a 'spirit' able to communicate with the group by means of paranormal rappings. The experiment has been repeated on a number of occasions, and there appears to be little doubt of its validity. It has been suggested that the experimenters, by their clear, detailed, and sustained thinking about the fictitious character Philip, created a 'thought form', a physical entity capable of producing sounds and other physical effects. The effects were weakened by the disbelief of

How nature evades attempts to observe her closely. Light passing through a slit spreads to form a patch of light on a screen (1). When a second slit is opened, an interference pattern of light and dark bands is formed where the two beams overlap (2). This can be explained by regarding each beam as a train of waves (3). Where they overlap, dark bands are formed at points where 'peaks' and 'troughs' cancel each other out (4). But other experiments show that light must also be viewed as made up of 'particles', called photons. In the one-slit experiment, each photon can follow a wide range of paths (5). But when the second slit is opened, certain paths are 'forbidden' – the photon cannot arrive in a dark band (6). But how can a photon travelling through one slit 'know' whether the other slit is open or closed? It seems that the photon 'goes through both slits at once' – it cannot be regarded as having a well-defined path in these circumstances

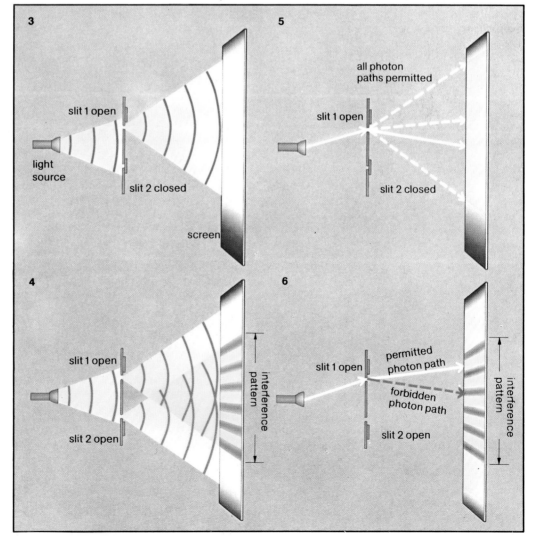

group members, and greatly strengthened by belief – even though this belief was of rather an unusual kind; for everyone in the group was well aware that they had 'made up' Philip.

What consequences for science in general follow from this? Suppose a scientist has a long-cherished belief in a particular physical theory, spends a great deal of time clarifying it in his mind and conducts experiments that are suggested by the theory; then it seems possible that physical effects confirming the theory can be *created* by this activity.

There are many cases of scientists who produced experimental results in accordance with some theory and were able to repeat them, while other workers were at first unable to do the same. This is usually attributed to the necessity for the other researchers to familiarise themselves with the experimental set-up and learn the skills necessary to conduct the experiment. But might it not also be that their own scepticism inhibited the effects that the original researcher achieved?

In some cases researchers have been unable to continue getting results, after an initial period of success. Could this be the result of discouragement by the unreceptive attitude of the scientific community?

Every year new, short-lived elementary particles are discovered. Frequently their existence is predicted before their discovery. It has been seriously suggested that these particles are being produced, rather than discovered, by the sustained mental efforts of physicists around the world. Although we have been conditioned to accept naïve realism by our scientifically based education, such an idea cannot be dismissed out of hand.

So naïve realism is an inadequate basis for an experiment in psychical matters. If the experiment involves the mind of a subject or subjects (and what experiment does not?) then it is essential to remember that the experimenter and any collaborators are parts

An indivisible whole

The amazing properties of the hologram are regarded by some scientists, such as David Bohm, as a vivid analogy for the indivisibility of the Universe. The hologram is a photograph of an object made by a special technique involving lasers. The light from a laser is of very pure colour – it has a single well-defined wavelength. The light waves are also very orderly – they are in phase, or 'in step' with each other. In making a hologram, no lens is used to form an image. Instead there is an apparently meaningless pattern of light and dark areas on the film. When the film is illuminated with laser light, however, a solid-looking image of the original object becomes visible (left, above). The film looks like a window through which the image is viewed; by shifting his viewpoint the observer can see details that are invisible from his original position. Ordinary stereoscopic photographs, by contrast, do not permit the viewer to 'look round the edge' of the image.

More strikingly still, cutting a small piece from the hologram and using that to form the image makes very little difference (left, below). The image loses some of its sharpness and must now be viewed through a smaller 'window' – but by shifting his position around, the observer can again view almost as much of the object as he could with the larger hologram.

Each small area of the hologram contains 'information', in 'coded' form, about the whole object, as seen from the position at which the hologram was made. That information is 'decoded' by the laser light to form a 'message' that is intelligible to us – the image. In a similar way, it may be that every object – or every mind – contains 'information' about the whole of the Universe – but in a coded form. Is this hidden unity of the Universe revealed when paranormal phenomena occur – and when the scientist discovers he is not separate from the Universe that he studies?

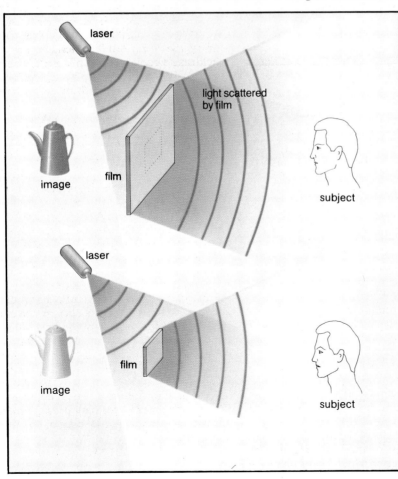

laser

light scattered by film

film

image

subject

laser

film

image

subject

of the experiment too. In fact, the subject, the experimental team, their beliefs and their attitude towards the theory they are testing, the equipment, the laboratory and the world beyond, form a gestalt, an organised whole. It seems to be impossible to draw hard and fast divisions between any of these and say that they cannot influence each other, even though, in certain circumstances, that influence may be very weak.

The idea that all human beings are part of a greater whole, and are therefore inextricably linked, is a very old one. But it has only recently found its way into science, and most present-day scientists do not yet accept it. We are all – in the West at any rate – conditioned from an early age to accept the very inadequate view that human beings are no more than a mass of complex tissues surmounted by a living micro-computer, and that we are all quite separate from each other and from the physical Universe in which we find ourselves. It is very difficult for us to

Top: paths of subatomic particles in a bubble chamber. The coiled tracks were produced by a stray cosmic ray; the roughly horizontal ones belong to artificially produced particles, which were the intended subjects of study. Is the intense thought devoted to these phenomena by the world's scientists actually helping to create them?

Above: Gertrude Schmeidler (centre), who found that the attitudes of subjects and researchers affect the success of experiments in parapsychology. Others have confirmed her work

accept the clear evidence that it is not so. 'We are members one of another,' wrote Paul, and teachers from all the world's great religions have agreed with him. The scientific evidence that this is literally true grows. But the well-conditioned scientist meeting this evidence immediately responds with a well-developed defence reaction. It is interesting to see most of his scientific objectivity fly out of the window as he struggles to reduce the 'cognitive dissonance' (psychologists' jargon for a real or supposed mismatch between a subject's perceptions and his ideas of the way things should be). The greatest scientists do not fly from unfamiliar ideas in this way: genius seems able to resist the conditioning process, or to discount it.

Western exponents of the idea that human beings and the rest of the Universe are one whole, the evidence of which keeps breaking through in so many ways, are not uncommon.

The eminent South African statesman Jan Christiaan Smuts put forward the idea in his writings on 'holism' – the doctrine that 'wholes are greater than the sum of their parts', having new properties that are not reducible to the properties of the parts. (The word 'holy' has the same root as 'holism' – denoting the idea of wholeness.)

The great psychologist C.G. Jung wrote about 'synchronicity' – the occurrence of meaningful patterns among things and events, inexplicable by cause and effect. The journalist Arthur Koestler in *The roots of coincidence* has championed these ideas and those of the biologist Paul Kammerer on 'the law of series'. This is the alleged occurrence of of meaningful coincidences in series of events more frequently than we would expect by chance. Later, Koestler co-authored a work on various aspects of ESP and synchronicity, *The challenge of chance*. The evidence produced by psychical researchers by no means stands alone.

Guided evolution

The most recent – and extremely controversial – evidence in this area is that presented by the biologist Rupert Sheldrake. He postulates the existence of 'morphogenetic fields' – non-physical structure-forming fields that carry biological 'information'. The development of an individual organism, and the evolution of a species, are guided by these fields, or memory pools. The response from that organ of the scientific establishment, *Nature*, was predictable in all but its intensity: the editor headed a leading article on Sheldrake's book with the phrase 'A book for burning?' The reaction of many physicists to David Bohm's ideas has been depressingly similar.

The response of scientific orthodoxy to both these theories has been very like its response to Einstein's work. The evidence in the case of relativity finally became so strong that it was irresistible. The theories of Einstein are now 'establishment science'. Perhaps in due course Bohm's theories will receive the same recognition; in the meantime, it is unfortunate that they have had the same reception that greeted Einstein's.

The experimenter effect is, then, a phenomenon that does not accord with the basis of most modern scientific practice. However, there appears to be little doubt that it exists and cannot be ignored. Its occurrence could have been foreseen from the teachings of various traditions, especially those of Eastern religion and philosophy, and now seems to be confirmed by the findings in various areas of science. There can be little doubt of its profound importance. The recognition of the experimenter effect may presage radical changes in our ways of looking at the world and at mankind.

Creator and creation are inextricably mixed in this arresting print by the Dutch artist M.C. Escher. A 'real' hand makes a drawing of a hand – which leaves the page, becomes 'real' and draws . . . the first hand. This is a striking metaphor for the emerging view of the Universe: the theories and beliefs of the scientist, apparently moulded by reality, become an important factor in shaping that reality

Cause and effect

Scientists' confidence might be shaken if they were forced to acknowledge that they are unwitting actors in their own experiments. But some have already had to face up to this possibility

NEW SCIENTIFIC THEORIES that do not seem to agree with what is thought to be known are frequently rejected without a careful examination. Innovators who have been able to overcome their own educational conditioning to create original ideas are obliged to put up with this sort of response from the scientific 'establishment' until the day when their ideas become generally accepted – and, probably, become a new orthodoxy. The idea that scientific investigators and their collaborators are an integral part of their own experiments is such an idea.

I had an experience of the inability of scientists to face this possibility in my own laboratory. I was studying a well-known British psychic. He was apparently creating paranormal physical effects in a complex apparatus in which an infra-red beam was produced and its intensity measured by electronic circuitry. The psychic was apparently able to cause a sudden drop in the reading indicating the beam's intensity. (Whether it was the beam's actual intensity or the measuring instrument that was affected is uncertain.) The effect was repeated a number of times and seemed so clear and definite that I fetched three colleagues who were not part

Brian Inglis, writer on the paranormal and consultant to *The Unexplained*, has come across examples of biological experiments in which success or failure apparently depended on psychic influences from the researcher

of the team, as independent witnesses. All fully understood the 'normal' electrical engineering and physics. They watched the effect being produced several times to order. Two of them were fascinated, declaring that they did not understand how it could possibly occur. They readily agreed to their names being quoted as witnesses. The third stated that 'there must be an explanation', even if he had not yet found it, and practically ran from the laboratory. He reduced the stress of this clash between what he was seeing with his own eyes and the received ideas of orthodoxy by refusing to admit the facts at all.

Every researcher knows of experiments that did not give the expected results; the phenomenon is very common. Usually it is assumed that something went wrong and the experiment is repeated until it does give the 'correct' result. One wonders how many research students who do not clearly understand what the result of an experiment is supposed to be produce anomalous results – sometimes by their own unrecognised psychic ability – and are told to repeat the procedure until they get a more acceptable result. Perhaps the spoon-bending children who appeared following Uri Geller's television shows were able to produce paranormal results because they did not know that they were impossible – at least, according to their physics teachers.

The psychical researcher Rhea White has

made the point forcefully:

the experimenter has been a neglected variable in parapsychological research. . . . There could hardly be a more significant area of investigation than the role of the experimenter, because not only may the achievement of extrachance results depend on the experimenter, but the experimenter may also affect the nature of the results obtained.

Perhaps the most important factor in successful experiments in psychical research is intense and sustained enthusiasm, and a desire on the part of the experimenter to get the best out of the subjects. This level of enthusiasm seemed to be present during the experiment with the British psychic mentioned above. It appears when the right people are present, and it must be carefully nurtured. Such an occasion is like a comet: its imminent arrival can be recognised, but it is not repeatable to order. The impressive paranormal events that can be brought about spring up and die down, and the skilful researcher must be ready for them – equipped to record them on audio- and videotape, and by other means, and to have witnesses present.

This phenomenon is by no means confined to psychical research. Brian Inglis describes the experience of the noted biologist Neil Miller. Miller wanted to find out whether rats could learn to control certain bodily functions – an ability that would upset conventional ideas about the workings of their nervous systems. With difficulty he found an assistant willing to collaborate on the experiments. They discovered that rats could indeed learn to alter blood pressure, heart rate, the temperature of one ear independently of the other, and other functions. Even though this sounded wildly improbable, other researchers were able to repeat the experiments and published their results during 1959.

Several years later Inglis visited Miller and discovered that he had been unable to repeat the results at this later date. The progressive decline of the results was inexplicable to Miller. He might have been completely discredited as a scientist if it had not been found in the 1960s that human beings could learn to control bodily functions, such as heart rate, previously thought to be completely automatic and independent of conscious control. Inglis suggests that psychic abilities of Miller or his assistant, or someone else involved in the experiment, might have played a role in his early success – and for some reason this ability declined subsequently.

A similar decline in experimental success occured with Albert Sabin, the discoverer of an oral polio vaccine. He thought he had obtained reliable evidence that the virus

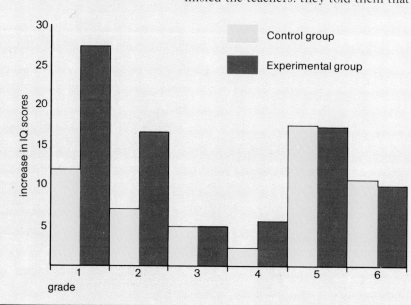

The favoured few

Psychologists are learning a great deal about the surprising ways in which human beings can influence the results obtained in supposedly objective tests. A classic demonstration was made by Robert Rosenthal and Lenore Jacobson in an American elementary school. They asked teachers to administer a nonverbal intelligence test to children in all six grades (ages 5 to 11). They then misled the teachers: they told them that the results indicated that certain children, who were named to the teachers, would show marked gains in their scores during the coming year. In reality these children had been selected randomly. They represented one fifth of all the pupils. Eight months later the teachers again administered the tests. The graph (left) shows the results. In all grades there was an average increase in test scores; but in grades 1 and 2 the children who had been marked out as promising made much greater gains than the rest. Some of the classes were tested by an educator from another school. She obtained the same results. In some unknown way the teachers' expectations about their pupils had called forth improved results.

Such effects can appear in very unexpected places. Before this work with schoolchildren, Rosenthal had studied behavioural scientists working with rats. Some researchers were told that their rats had been bred for intelligence; others were told that theirs had been bred for dullness. The results they obtained in such apparently straightforward tests as maze-running confirmed the supposed brightness or stupidity of the rats – which were, of course, a randomly selected sample.

increase in IQ scores — grade

Control group
Experimental group

that causes herpes also caused many human cancers. Later he was quite unable to obtain the same results.

There are many examples of carefully controlled scientific trials that have produced such strongly conflicting results that the effects of the experimenters' beliefs and attitudes must be seriously considered. The best known data on the effects of the experimenters' expectations about the outcomes of the experiment were provided by Robert Rosenthal in 1966. They are widely quoted, but also widely criticised. However, he makes it clear that careful thought must go into the design of experiments in human behaviour, and experimental psychologists must be suspected of the same kinds of errors as parapsychologists.

An interesting study was carried out by the American parapsychologist J.C. Crumbaugh in 1958. He had been unsuccessful in his attempts to demonstrate paranormal effects and had decided that the personality of the experimenter must be an important factor. With the help of the staff at the Parapsychology Laboratory at Duke University, North Carolina, he designed a series of experiments. He worked with 16 subjects and 16 experimenters, working in long and short sessions. He studied the personalities and attitudes of both subjects and experimenters, and rated them according to their degree of self-confidence or insecurity, and their degree of belief or disbelief in ESP. He obtained results in the expected direction – that is, with the self-confident participants who believed in the possibility of success. He then refined the experimental design and

Albert B. Sabin shows how his polio vaccine is administered. At one time Sabin thought he had demonstrated that certain human cancers are carried by viruses; but after a while he found himself unable to obtain the same experimental results. Was the change due to random disturbances – or to some change in his own attitude to his work?

repeated it, using only long sessions. No significant ESP results showed up.

Nevertheless, though he used 16 experimenters, Crumbaugh remained the principal experimenter: it is still possible that his own conviction that he could not succeed in ESP experiments inhibited his results. For there is no doubt that different experimenters obtain different results in similar psi tests.

Brian Inglis delivered the J.B. Rhine lecture to the Parapsychological Association in 1980. Its theme was of great importance in this area. His title was: 'Power corrupts; scepticism corrodes'. Many parapsychologists tend to be sceptical of the existence of the phenomena they study, though often

Getting the drift

When Einstein's theory of relativity became the orthodoxy of the scientific world, conflicting theories and experiments had difficulty in gaining a hearing – just as relativity itself had at first been rejected as inconceivable. The most distinguished physicist to bring contrary evidence was an American, Dayton C. Miller. He repeated the experiment of A.A. Michelson and E.W. Morley, first performed in 1887, which had come to be regarded as the cornerstone of the experimental evidence for relativity. It involved comparing the time of travel of two light beams along different paths. When Michelson and Morley performed the experiment, they expected that the 'wind' of ether (the hypothetical medium in which light waves travelled) would affect a beam travelling parallel to the Earth's motion more severely than a beam travelling at right angles to it. But they could find no difference, and it was gradually accepted that the ether does not exist.

From 1921 to 1926 Miller repeatedly carried out the Michelson-Morley experiment. His results varied – but he was convinced that they revealed an 'ether wind' with a speed of about 6 miles per second (10 kilometres per second) – one third of the Earth's speed around the Sun.

This work was sufficiently respected to win Miller a prize of $1000 from the American Academy of Sciences. No one had demonstrated any flaw in it by the time of Miller's death in 1941. But the implication that ether drift was detectable was rejected. Other experiments supported relativity, and in due course the Michelson-Morley experiment was repeated with other types of radiation, such as radio and radar, with no sign of ether drift.

In the 1950s Miller's results were closely analysed, and the investigators concluded that his results had been partly due to temperature fluctuations and partly due to random disturbances. But long before this reasoned criticism was made, the mass of scientists had assumed that something 'must' be wrong with such heretical results.

they are quite unconscious of this resistance. Consequently they refuse to accept almost any effect, no matter how unequivocal the evidence for it, for fear of being 'conned'.

The orthodox scientist will protest at this point. 'This is manifest nonsense!' he will say. 'You are suggesting that whatever non-sensical pseudo-scientific idea anyone comes up with is verifiable!'

Not at all: this does not necessarily follow. Take the morphogenetic field (or memory pool) as an example. The field was postulated to explain the course of past evolution, and the development of living individuals throughout the course of their lives. These processes existed long before there was any Rupert Sheldrake to propose the existence of the field. But if its existence is confirmed at some future date, it will be by the demonstration of further effects and properties of the field manifesting themselves in new experimental arrangements. And it may be that, initially, some experimenters are more successful in demonstrating it than others. It is possible that these discoveries will not be made until scientific thinking is substantially in accord with them, when there will be a great weight of detailed thinking behind the notion of the morphogenetic field.

The opinions prevailing among the non-scientific public may also be highly important in determining what experimental results can be obtained. And these can be swayed by the opinions of noted scientists. However, it is probably the whole formed by the subjects and the experimenter that is of primary importance.

Patterns of guessing

There are, of course, ways in which the attitudes and beliefs of experimenters and subjects can influence the results without involving paranormal agencies. Subjects frequently tend to avoid calling the same card twice in a row during card-guessing experiments. This may be a quite unconscious habit, or it may be due to a belief that 'lightning doesn't strike twice in the same place'. In fact, if the drawing of the cards is truly random, all cards are equally likely to be drawn on any occasion, no matter what the previous card has been (provided each card is returned to the pack before the next draw). Someone else might have a preference for calling a particular type of card, and so on. If the card-drawing is not completely random, the biases of the subject may result in scores that are significantly above or below those that would be expected by pure chance – even if no paranormal factor is involved.

There is a tragic and highly controversial example of what may be an unusual case of the experimenter effect. The important experiments of S.G. Soal, a former president of the British Society for Psychical Research, have been widely regarded as outstanding in their class. They were card-guessing experiments that apparently demonstrated the

Top: S.G. Soal conducted a classic series of experiments apparently demonstrating the existence of telepathy. But he had altered certain figures in his results, thus giving his subjects a spuriously high success rate

Above: J.B. Rhine and his wife Louisa. The most impressive demonstrations of ESP by the Rhines occurred early in their career, when, as J.B. Rhine believed, their enthusiasm was at its height

existence of telepathy. A later computer analysis of his results indicated that the figure 1 had been altered to 4 or 5 in various places. Subsequently an independent observer at Soal's experiments claimed that she had seen him making this kind of illicit alterations.

This was a shattering discovery to para-psychologists. Some of them have seriously suggested that an alternative to conscious fraud is possible. The changes may have been made quite unwittingly by Soal: his subconscious mind may have seized on this as a way of obtaining the results that he so passionately desired.

Cynics will scoff at this explanation, of course. They will classify Soal with those physical mediums who have been caught cheating when supposedly in trance during seances. But I am fairly sure that in at least some cases these mediums too were not cheating consciously and deliberately: they were in an 'altered state of consciousness', in which their normal mind was not in control.

Of course, it is deplorable that the experimental conditions during these seances and during Soal's experiments were so faulty that this 'cheating' could take place. We are learning rapidly, and the rate of learning is increasing. We can now record the activities of all participants in an experiment, and analyse the results completely automatically, thus circumventing most of these earlier difficulties. Thus the enthusiasm and optimism of experimenters and subjects are able to contribute to the success of the experiment, without distorting the results.

What the psychical researchers are bringing out – and this is perhaps the special importance of the topic – is the influence of human views and expectations in *all* experiments. This factor may well be the explanation of the anomalous results that do not find their way into the orthodox scientific literature. Gradually it is being appreciated by scientists – but not yet sufficiently.

Index